D1409493

beyond
the great
divide

JUDITH GILL After teaching in high schools in Australia and the United States, Judith Gill returned to university to study gender issues in educational practice. Her doctoral work on gender construction in schooling involved comparing environments in single-sex and coeducational high schools. In the late 1980s, through the Projects of National Significance scheme, she published an overview of the research on the question of single-sex versus coeducation and has since been involved in numerous presentations, publications and consultancies on this issue.

To all those who teach,

Wherever they work, in whatever capacity,

Be it as parents, professionals, artisans, elders or just friends,

And to all those who seek to become teachers,

In acknowledgement of our mutual desire

To make the world a fairer place.

beyond the great divide

single sex or coeducation?

JUDITH GILL

UNSW PRESS

A UNSW PRESS BOOK

Published by
University of New South Wales Press Ltd
University of New South Wales
Sydney NSW 2052
AUSTRALIA
www.unswpress.com.au

National Library of Australia
Cataloguing-in-Publication entry

Gill, Judith.
Beyond the great divide: coeducation or single-sex?

Bibliography.
Includes index.
ISBN 0 86840 614 7.

1. Coeducation – Australia. 2. Girls – Education -
Australia. 3. Boys – Education – Australia. 4. Sex
differences in education – Australia. I. Title.

371.82

Cover design and image Di Quick
Printer Hyde Park Press

CONTENTS

PREFACE

One of the singular and striking features of the Australian landmass is the line of mountains that runs parallel to the eastern coast. It is called the Great Dividing Range – largely because of the natural barriers these mountains posed to the pioneers in the early days of white settlement, thereby dividing the 'civilised' settled areas along the coast from the wild, untamed and unruly outback. The concept of the 'great divide' has been used by some educational researchers as a metaphor – most notably by Clark (1989) – to describe the ways in which schooling typically forges distinctions between male and female, boys and girls. (Where other analysts have used the term 'gap', along with 'divide', to frame the debates around gender and schooling, the deliberate choice of the 'Great Divide' for an Australian readership indicates the need for discussions about education to be connected to their physical and cultural context.) This book will urge educators and parents to work against the construction of unnecessary barriers to children's learning and to work together for a more inclusive society.

The book originated with the idea of provoking some clear thinking about the ways in which schooling in Australia prepares young people to enter the world as productive and engaged citizens, in keeping with the official statement of the national goals of schooling, which has come to be known as the 'Adelaide Declaration'. This statement affirmed that:

> Australia's future depends upon each citizen having the necessary knowledge, understanding, skills and values for a productive and rewarding life in an educated, just and open society.

In particular, this declaration affirmed the principle of social justice in schooling by requiring that:

> Schooling should be socially just, so that:
> 3.1 students' outcomes from schooling are free from the effects

of negative forms of discrimination based on sex, language, culture and ethnicity, religion or disability; and of differences arising from students' socio-economic background or geographic location. (MCEETYA 1999, p. 4)

Some of the issues covered in the following pages will sketch aspects of schooling that led the Ministerial Committee to take up this position. In particular, this book will look at gender construction in schooling practice and relate this process to the research on the effect of schools operating in differing gender contexts, such as being organised as single-sex institutions and classes or coeducational ones. This book starts from the conviction that, despite some conscious efforts to be newly challenging, such as the progressive education movement in the 1960s and 1970s, schooling has been and continues to be typically institutionalised in traditional ways. As some pundits have noted, running a schooling system can be compared to 'driving by looking in the rear vision mirror', because we are continually looking backwards in the attempt to see where we should be heading. Take for instance the debates around standards, which reappear with monotonous regularity. Questions are raised such as: Do Year 3 children today possess the same measurable skills as they had twenty years ago? How much algebra do school students understand before they stop taking mathematics courses? Such questions are often accompanied by laments like: 'In my day we all learned how to spell!' and 'Discipline isn't like what it used to be'. Much of this can be dismissed as time-honoured laments about 'young people today', which have been a recurring feature of recorded history. Noting how the school is too often blamed for various social ills, British educationist John Beck writes:

> Claims that the nation is in decline seem never ending: the economy, family life, moral standards, a sense of community, the nation's health, even our national sporting achievements – all these have been identified as areas where things are getting progressively worse. Although a moment's thought makes it highly implausible that educational institutions could really be responsible for so much decay, they have, nevertheless, been recurrently targeted and held responsible. (Beck 1998, p. 1)

And so it is not just Australian schools that are blamed for a range of social ills. Yet surely some of these concerns are valid and justifiable. We want our young people to learn about the society in which they live and to be taught to value the things that we, the older generation, value. And sometimes we delight in the fact that modern technology appears to support this learning more surely and more quickly than was our own experience.

However, education does have a built-in time lag, which is perhaps inevitable. Like just about every other known society we tend to educate our young people in varying approximations of the ways in which we ourselves were educated. While very few of us make choices about schooling for our children on the basis of what was most like our own experience – and some of us deliberately choose places that are as different as we can imagine from those harsh locations of childhood memories – in a range of ways we tend to reproduce the culture of childhood along the lines of the way we were ourselves formed.

This process of looking backwards can make it quite difficult for schools to adjust to social and cultural change. After all, teachers are charged with the responsibility to prepare the new generation with an understanding of the culture of the parent generation and, at the same time, to provide the skills whereby students can analyse and participate in the culture and society of the present. These days cultural change is particularly dynamic given the computer driven speed of data manipulation and transmission and continual new developments in communications technology. In this 'information society', social and cultural change is an ongoing feature of the life worlds of all of us. Hence it must also be part of the teaching and learning in school.

Along with the rest of the Western world, one of the most significant cultural changes that has occurred here in Australia during recent decades has been the increased participation of women in all levels of public life, most especially in the area of paid work. There has been a subsequent great increase in public awareness of issues relating to girls and women in terms of their education and life chances. The girls in school today are destined for lives very different from those of their grandmothers' generation and in many cases also considerably different from their mothers' experiences. Such changes, though profound, did not appear overnight but rather have been part of an ongoing movement in Western society.

During the late twentieth century, in Australia several significant constitutional achievements supported the broader engagement of increasing numbers of women in the public world. These included the removal of the marriage bar for women in the Public Service in 1966 (before this time, women were required to resign on marriage) and the passage of the *Equal Opportunity Acts* enshrining the principle of equal pay for equal work. The work of the federal Affirmative Action Agency provided ongoing support for women's equality in the workplace. Today, Australian women are in many respects more equal to their male counterparts than at any other previous time. More women are working beyond the home and the majority of young women envisage being in paid work for most of their adult lives. Although women are still in the minority at the highest levels of business and government, more of them are in paid work, in tertiary education and in powerful positions in the public sphere. Not surprisingly, the latest United Nations accounting of women's status across a range of countries identified Australia as the most desirable place in the world to live if you are a woman (Haslem 2002). There are evident implications for the educational experience of all our young people in the process of preparing them for a world significantly different from that of their parents' generation.

At the beginning of the twenty-first century we as a society are less gender divided than ever before. This does not mean that gender distinction has disappeared, however – far from it. The following chapters will examine the ways in which schooling arrangements have adjusted to these profound social changes and will look particularly at the question of school gender context within the whole debate.

Outline of the argument

The introduction to this book sets up a key theme, namely that considerations of education must always be cognisant of the particular contexts in which students and schools are located. Thus, although many features of Australian educational systems have fairly clearly grown out of the British system, it would be wrong to imagine that answers to educational questions that work for British schools will apply in the same way in Australia. Even more doubtful are propositions that come from other countries whose educational systems are even more different from our own. The Introduction traces broad features of the gender issue in Australian education.

Chapter 1 introduces its central question, the relation between gender and education in terms of a brief overview of the history of Australian education, noting that gender was absent from much educational thinking until the 1970s when it became a key area of research and debate.

The second chapter contextualises concerns about the education of girls in terms of Australian educational provisions. A review of the research on girls and education is presented with particular attention to the ways in which the focus on girls changes through the decades following the 1975 interim report of the Commonwealth Schools Commission, *Girls, School and Society*, which signalled the government's initial commitment to gender equity in education.

The focus changes in the third chapter to the current debates about boys and education. Here the differences between the agenda for the girls and education movement and the more recent boys' education lobby are summarised. A key point in this discussion is that research in the area of boys' education is divided between, on the one hand, well-theorised accounts of the discursive production of certain sorts of masculinity in schooling practice and, on the other, a series of claims and grievances that, despite being well rehearsed, are not grounded in documented study.

Chapter 4 surveys the research on the relative merits of single-sex schooling compared with coeducation from an Australian perspective. Several different lines of research are discussed, and the difficulty of finding the solution to the question: Which way to school? is identified. At the same time the existing research is useful in that it helps reframe the question in particular ways. The chapter concludes by pointing out that the question of the impact of school gender contexts and their effects on schooling outcomes will always and only be answerable in terms of the broader culture and the particular historical moment.

The fifth chapter surveys international research on the issue of single-sex schooling as compared with coeducation and shows that a similar range of issues has arisen in the United States and the United Kingdom to those in Australia. However, the dimensions of these issues vary in terms of location. In the United Kingdom, for example, a stronger history of schooling divided into a small section of elite academic schools and a larger section of generalist educational institutions has caused higher degrees of anxiety than in Australia. In the United States the all-encompassing tradition of mixed schooling enshrined in law has meant that the question of school gender context has arisen only recently and mainly in particular school systems which are themselves subsets of mainstream schooling.

The final chapter attempts to synthesise the thinking on gender and education from an Australian perspective in terms of the question of school gender context. Ultimately, as in so many educational discussions, the usefulness of the question of school gender context relates to the fact that in addressing it one has to grapple with questions about the purpose of education and its relation to schooling and the wider society.

ACKNOWLEDGMENTS

I have been supported in this writing by friends and colleagues at the University of South Australia. I thank them all for their cheerful daily interactions and their continuing willingness to engage in ongoing discussion about key elements of the arguments presented here. In addition I want to make mention of the vibrant group of research students whose passions about education and about research, in equal measure, have fortified my own deliberations and energised my thinking. In particular, I have been grateful for the help of one of these, Deborah Tranter, whose careful close reading has helped convert my tendency to ramble into a more or less coherent whole. Any mistakes remaining are, of course, all my own.

Lastly I want to acknowledge my indebtedness to the Research Centre for Gender Studies and to the School of Education at the University of South Australia, both of which have provided a home base for my work within the wider University context. Colleagues from both these groups and fellow members of the Australian Association for Research in Education have supplied me with a constant stream of ideas and encouragement.

Judith Gill
Underdale Campus, University of South Australia, 2004

INTRODUCTION

It is around 3 pm on a grey Sunday in London in early spring. I wander through the lovely old church on the corner in High Street, Kensington – surely one of the world's best-known churches, if not exactly the most frequented. The busy throng of Kensington High Street forms a constant stream, even on Sunday. During the week the front of the church appears to be used as a common meeting point for passers-by, with many of the local workers using the seats in the adjoining garden to sit and have a quick bite of lunch or a snatched cup of coffee and a cigarette. Inside, the church is quiet, dim and stately – the peace of the place contrasting starkly with the busyness of the outside world. I notice the memorial to a nineteenth-century explorer of the Kimberleys in Western Australia who was born and raised in the Kensington parish. The memorial serves as one example of the ways in which attitudes and practices from Imperial Britain spread to the other side of the world. Another is schooling itself. The desire to find – in the schoolbooks they used to say *discover,* thereby signifying no previous legitimate human existence – and name distant parts of the world for England was no doubt seeded in the education systems of those earlier times. Many of the celebrated explorers of this country were educated in England in schools that later became models for schooling in Australia. One recurring theme of this book – and indeed of most of the research on gender and schooling – will be the ways in which a particular schooling experience predisposes students for engagement with the world beyond school.

Beside the church itself and farthest away from the busy Kensington High Street stand the buildings that once housed the parish school. Over the large entry there are graceful letters carved in the old stone that proclaim BOYS. Slightly to the left another set of letters carved above a smaller, lower and less-imposing door carry the message GIRLS and INFANTS, showing that this lesser gateway was the path of entry to these evidently less-important participants in the school's educational experiences.

History records that, until relatively recently, social expectations of girls were very different from those of boys, especially regarding education. In many Western countries it was not until the late twentieth century that educationists began to review the different ways in which schooling worked to construct sex differences. By routinely separating girls and boys in a myriad of ways, schools thereby confirmed them as separate and distinct, a distinction that education systems maintained long after the notions of separate abilities had been thoroughly discredited. There can be no doubt that schools once operated in a manner consistent with entrenched cultural beliefs about gender difference – and indeed, in varying degrees, that they still do. Having said that, the question remains: If schools once operated in non-inclusive ways with respect to gender, do they still have to? If so, to what degree? And why should teachers, parents and educators be concerned about it?

Returning to Kensington High Street on a week day, I discover that a school still functions in the old buildings. However, the smaller door for girls and infants is blocked off now and all the pupils enter through the big one marked BOYS – they tell me that no-one takes any notice of the old stone carvings and that it is simply the school door. I find it hard to believe that the daily procession past a sign such as this can be quite so readily dismissed, especially in the minds of young people who only recently have been taught how to decipher letters and grasp meaning from print. And while the teachers, parents and school administrators who also enter through that door may believe that the old stone signage is just a part of the heritage building decorations, I also wonder at the degree to which they are involved in making some sort of gender distinctions in their parenting, their teaching and their management practices which reflect some of those earlier educational traditions.

In reflecting in this vein I am reminded of the 1996 ABC documentary 'The First Day', which recorded the first day at school experiences for some fourteen children from varying parts of Australia. In each case one of the first pieces of learning and teacher direction for all the new school children concerned the important message about the location of the toilets, accompanied, at all the mixed schools, by a clear directive that girls use this one and boys go over there. The degree to which this learning – of essential separation between boys and girls, men and women – is reflected in the curriculum and practices of typical Australian school experience has long been taken for granted as part of the way we 'do' schooling in this country. And, despite some thirty years of critique of gender construction in schooling on the basis of the unnecessary limitations it can have on the process of individual learning, a good deal of it still goes on. Of course we no longer routinely require girls and boys to enter the school through separate doors, to play in different areas, to adhere to the 'line down the middle of the playground', to undertake very different subjects and study areas, but in many ways schooling remains a gendered experience for young Australians, whether they attend mixed or single-sex schools and classrooms. Just how much these gendered features impede the full development of each individual has been a recurring theme in the research on gender and schooling.

Within the general understanding of the role of the school in constructing gender, the question of the impact of school gender context – whether the school is mixed or single-sex – raises some very particular issues. While some see single-sex schools as 'the most fundamental expression of differing sex expectations' (Commonwealth Schools Commission, 1975, p. 63), others argue that such schools offer young people the freedom to be themselves, unhampered by societal expectations of gender conformity. For instance, prominent educational publicist Dale Spender wrote:

> When girls are educated in a context from which boys are absent, in which they are encouraged to grow and develop their human potential, then they will be in a much stronger position to resist oppression in the wider society. (Spender 1980, p. 65)

Between 1970 and 1990 the most common argument proposed in favour of single-sex schooling was couched in these terms, namely that only in the experience of sex-segregated education can young people be in a position to achieve self-realisation unencumbered by gender stereotyping and pressure towards typical male and female roles. At this time the argument was put most powerfully and consistently in favour of girls schools – as noted in the Spender quotation above. Boys schools rarely rated a mention in this literature – other than as bastions of male privilege.

This call for girls-only schooling rapidly became a recurring theme in the Australian popular press and was particularly taken up by the highly articulate and vocal girls school lobby, the keenest proponents of which are located in and around Melbourne. Their much-repeated claim is that there is a need for a girls-only environment if girls are to succeed academically – even that girls can only learn in an all-girls environment. Certainly one effect of these calls has been that considerable numbers of middle-class parents are convinced of the virtues of girls-only schooling for their daughters. For many, this preference means paying for their daughter's education at one of the non-government single-sex girls schools. Only in New South Wales are there still significant numbers of publicly funded girls schools. Recently several selective entry mixed high schools in Sydney reported having trouble filling their classes with appropriate numbers of bright girls because so many of the girls' parents preferred an all-girls school for their daughters, even if that school were non-selective entry. Similarly, in other states, selective entry mixed schools have become accustomed to 'losing' significant numbers of their girls who have won scholarships to private girls schools early in their secondary schooling.

Over two-thirds of Australian school children currently experience all their schooling in mixed schools; the proportion of students at primary level in mixed schools is higher than at the secondary level. This is particularly true of the government sector, most of whose schools are comprehensively patterned to cater to the broadest range of students. There are still some selective entry government high schools (most of these are in New South Wales) and some few government single-sex schools (again most in New South Wales), but the main pattern is mixed ability and coeducation. The non-government sector too is becoming more aligned with coeducation than once was the case. A clear majority of the newer schools are organised along coeducational lines and it is noteworthy that schools that have changed from single-sex to coeducation have been more commonly schools that were previously boys-only establishments. The adoption of coeducation by former girls schools is less common. While some of the oldest established boys schools continue to serve their particular communities in their traditional ways, there has been a clear trend towards coeducation in many of the established boys schools around the country. The reasons given for this development are often a mix of educational argument, market forces, parental choice and economic imperatives.

To make matters more complicated, the last ten years have also seen an upsurge of interest in the educational needs of boys – which of course is itself an assumption that such needs are both identifiable and distinct from the educational needs of girls. Whereas the girls in education movement had initially campaigned so that girls' education would be more like that of boys – so that girls could complete secondary schooling, do the prestigious subjects of maths and science, take on positions of influence such as school captain and so on – the boys' education lobby appears to ask that boys' education be constructed differently from that of girls. Some of the lobbyists for boys' education as an area of special need argue that boys need the experience of male-only groupings in order to affirm their identity as young men. They bemoan the demise of boys-only schools and have continued to lobby for more attention to the needs of boys. This sentiment was expressed very forcefully by the headmaster of one boys school in 1993:

> When one looks at the statistics in Australia, one realises how bereft of educational rationale the move to coeducation has been. In the last twenty-five years, forty Australian independent schools have turned coeducational, thirty-seven of whom have been boys' schools and of the remaining three one has since gone out of existence. This is no commitment to coeducation. The girls' schools have, after all, stood firm. It reflects more a creeping loss of confidence in how to be a successful school for boys in contemporary Australian society. (Hutchins School 1993, p. 4)

The speaker's vehement commitment to a separate and specialist education for boys underpins his every word – so much so that schools who chose otherwise are described as having 'turned', a term that mixes sentiments of faith and loyalty and their antonyms – lack of faith, treason – in the minds of the readers. His claim that the move to coeducation runs counter to the real educational interests of boys is not supported by any evidence other than tradition bolstered by his own conviction.

So many claims – but where is the evidence? This book offers an integrated account of the research evidence and the popular positions on these questions. It begins with a historical overview of the development of Australian schooling with relation to gender and proceeds to an analysis of the arguments for separate schooling for both girls and boys. In the concluding chapters it puts forward the suggestion that the question of gender and schooling is properly one that should keep recurring, as it is itself a sort of gold standard by which our schools can be ranked on a continuum from inclusivity through to exclusion. Only after looking at the evidence can parents, teachers, education students and members of the wider community be reasonably expected to make rational decisions about their own position on single-sex schooling. Such decisions are of course not always rational – even more seldom are they solely rational, more often invested with hopes and dreams and the weight of accumulated cultural knowledge. In the end all we can hope for is to have produced more evidence about the question in order to help people build the sort of society in which we can all participate without fear or favour. Such is surely the ultimate goal of education.

1

WHY ARE OUR SCHOOLS THE WAY THEY ARE?

Overview
This chapter provides a brief historical overview of education in Australia, noting especially the educational implications of social changes in the late twentieth century. In this account particular attention is given to the absence and then presence of issues around gender.

Nearly thirty years ago at Cornell University in Ithaca, New York, I came across the work of Urie Bronfenbrenner who was working on an investigation into the ways in which the different cultural contexts in which children were raised impacted on their learning experiences. In one publication he contrasted the differing 'worlds' experienced by children living in the United States with those in what was then the USSR. Later he included a study of children in Japan. The lesson I took from this work was encapsulated in a video made about his studies titled *Worlds of Childhood*. The images shown were of preschool children: first a racially mixed group in a typical North American nursery school, complete with the latest educational toys and bright wall posters; the scene then moved to a Scandinavian nursery where individual fair-haired, blue-eyed children played with wooden toys painted in bright colours in scenes that appeared to be straight out of the delightful children's books of Dick Bruna; following this we were shown an overcrowded (to Western eyes) nursery in China with children inside playpens without any toys at all, just lots and lots of other children. In each case the children appeared busy, happy and contented. Even the most casual viewer must have noted the striking environmental differences between the children's locations. In each case the children's environments reflected the differing cultures, values and attitudes in which they were being raised. This point was particularly relevant to me, a visiting Australian teacher who was very conscious of the social and cultural differences between American school environments and the ones in which I had been working in Australia.

When we live and raise our children within the one culture there is a tendency to suppose that the ways things are done are simple responses to children's needs. But of course this is only part of the picture. Bronfenbrenner's work was to amplify over and over again the simple truth that childrearing offers a window onto a cultural world more surely than just about any other cultural practice. Schooling, too, typically reflects the values and practices of the culture in which it is embedded, at the same time as it ensures those attitudes and values will be reproduced in subsequent generations. It is instructive to look at the case of Australian education in this regard.

Education only for the wealthy

In the early days of the Australian colonies education functioned as a private good and was restricted to those who could pay for their children to be schooled, either at home with a governess or through some form of institutional arrangement. Within the latter category there was still a broad range of offerings, from the Dame schools set up in private houses to the prestigious private boys schools such as the Collegiate School of St Peter founded in 1847 in Adelaide, Sydney Grammar (1857), Melbourne Grammar (1858) or Brisbane Grammar (1869). At the other end of the spectrum, the Dame schools were generally run in their own homes by women without other means of support and sometimes of dubious educational qualifications. In general they did not survive the establishment of free public schooling, in direct contrast to the prestigious private boys schools, significant ones of which still exist today (such as those mentioned above).

These early boys schools were developed for the sons of wealthy colonials and their curricula and organisation mirrored those of the English Public Schools.[1] Students were routinely taught British History, English Literature, Latin and Mathematics, subjects that were standard in English schools at the time. Respect for Empire and all things British was written into all aspects of the curriculum at these schools. The majority of headmasters for such schools were Englishmen, often ministers of religion, who 'came out' for their term of office and then 'went home' when it was ended. Janet McCalman (1993, p. 60) writes of one such school which, during World War I, was ready to pride itself on having 'the longest list of war dead of any Australian school'. Another such school routinely listed the boys who had been killed as 'giving their lives for the school and for England', thereby eliding the idea of their being Australian at all. These stories provide some indication of the degree to which 'good' schooling, masculinity, patriotism and allegiance to all things British were intertwined in Australian colonial schooldays. Initially these schools provided virtually the only route for young Australians to attend the universities which had been established in the major cities. The current 'Group of Eight' 'sandstone' universities comprises several of these early elite institutions, although by now of course the tertiary sector encompasses some thirty more recent universities and accommodates a much broader range of students.

Schooling for the masses

In the late nineteenth century, the advent of mass schooling subsequent to the passing of the *Education Acts* provided free, compulsory and secular education for the children of the various colonies, and was to see the beginning of an education system in each of the soon-to-be Australian states and territories. Through the twentieth century this public education system became widely known as the 'state school system', especially in the eastern states, a name which recognises the fact that schooling came under state control rather than being subsumed by the federal government. To this day there are ongoing debates about the rights and responsibilities of the states in relation to the determination of educational policy and funding, a recurring impediment to the recent federal government efforts to develop a 'national education system'.

Once the *Acts* were passed in the late nineteenth century, free public education was theoretically available to all young Australians. However, in practice, it was more readily available to those who lived in the cities and sizeable country towns. From the beginning the free places were taken up more commonly by boys – parents being apparently much more ready to countenance keeping daughters at home to help with the work of the house, including care of younger brothers and sisters. Meanwhile, at school the children were separated by sex for much of their learning, a system that ensured that girls learned needlework and housewifely arts while boys were engaged with basic skills of woodwork and joinery (Miller 1986).

Essentially at this time education comprised the years of primary schooling; secondary schooling was not widely available within the state school systems until the second half of the twentieth century. Writing of the situation in South Australia, Miller notes: 'For nearly forty years Adelaide, Norwood, Unley and Woodville high schools were the only state high schools in the metropolitan area of Adelaide; only in the 1950s were new academic high schools added to the list' (Miller 1986, p. 137). This situation was mirrored in the other states, with few government high schools and most of them in the capital cities. Before the 1950s the vast majority of young Australians left school without any experience of the senior years of high school. Those who did undertake this level of education were likely to be in fee-paying schools and hence to come from the more privileged social group. They were also more likely to be boys. While there was a system of Workingmen's Institutes (later to become TAFE) that catered to the need for apprenticeships and trade skills for young Australian men, the numbers who went on to university were very few indeed. Hence, even though Australian universities had opened their doors to women by the late nineteenth century in advance of the British universities, for the first half of the last century the numbers of women able to take up higher education were very small due to the particular structures of schooling that governed entry.

A dual education system

In each state in the early twentieth century the dual system flourished – the established private schools catering to the educational needs of the children of the wealthy and the public schools open to all comers.[2] Interestingly enough, the desire of middle-class parents to educate their daughters to similar levels as their sons (although this did not mean they studied the same subjects!) brought about a press for the state to enter into the provision of secondary education. In Adelaide in 1879 the Advanced School for Girls, a fee-paying, albeit government-provided, secondary school for girls, offered just such a venture. The Adelaide Advanced School for Girls was not free, however its fees were relatively low and there was a system of bursaries available to be won by bright girls whose families could not afford the tuition. Mackinnon (1986) has documented the outstanding success of some of its early women graduates, many of whom went on to study at the University of Adelaide and achieve highly across a range of academic endeavours. The fact that it was a girls school was accountable mainly because there was an insufficient supply of academic education for girls at the time, rather than a deliberate philosophy of single-sex schooling. There were several non-government girls schools already in existence but these tended to offer a curriculum in which 'polite accomplishments' figured much more prominently than intellectually rigorous subjects. It is significant that several of the early women graduates of the University of Adelaide in the fields of science and medicine came directly from the Adelaide Advanced School for Girls as it did offer the girls an education which prepared them for further study.[3]

The fact that Australian universities admitted women to degree courses much earlier than did their British counterparts may well have been partly due to the need to build student numbers, given the very small proportion of the male population to achieve university entrance at the time. Even so, the women at university experienced significant levels of marginalisation from the generally male student body and the all-male faculty (Mackinnon 1986). There appears to have been a real reluctance in the university faculty members to recognise the presence of women students. Hence the apocryphal story of the Foundation Professor of English at the University of Sydney who routinely greeted the class with 'Gentlemen ...' thereby pointedly ignoring the women who sat in their designated seats in the first two rows. No doubt such habits reflected a training in the all-male British universities from whence the majority of university posts were filled.

The Adelaide Advanced School for Girls did not set out to be a girls school because of a conviction that the educational needs of girls were different to those of boys. If anything its founders' position would have been that girls' needs were very similar to those of their brothers – and unmet within the educational establishments of the time. The fact remains that this first government secondary school for girls was connected to high academic achievement and was a single-sex school. Girls schools in other states were soon to follow the achievements of the Adelaide Advanced School for Girls. As the twentieth century progressed, private girls schools across the states gradually undertook to offer more academic subjects to those girls who wanted to study them – while of course maintaining their diet of polite accomplishments for those whose tastes were along traditional lines. Not surprisingly then, throughout the first half of the twentieth century the girls who did achieve highly at school and went on to university had virtually all come from single-sex girls schools. The association between female achievement and single-sex schooling had become a clear feature in the history of Australian education.

Public secondary education

In all states the second half of the twentieth century saw a rapid expansion in government schooling at secondary level. While most state systems initially included some single-sex high schools, the majority were coeducational, as were the public primary schools. Public secondary education in the 1950s was divided between the high schools and the technical schools, the latter being aimed at providing young people with the necessary skills for gaining apprenticeships or other forms of entry to the workforce. Most of the technical schools were single-sex, reflecting the highly gender-divided labour force at the time. The girls technical schools ran classes in domestic science, typing and shorthand, and home management, while the boys' technical schools offered a wide range of woodwork, metalwork and basic mechanics courses. Many, though not all, of the technical schools were under resourced compared with the high schools. Although there were some important variations, in general very few students in the technical schools remained at school for the senior years.

Effectively many of these schools operated as second-class systems within the state educational provision. In Victoria a committee set up to investigate the technical school system in the late 1970s recommended the immediate 'disestablishment' (closure) of the girls technical schools, citing their lack of facilities, their low-grade educational offerings and their impossibly overcrowded conditions as rendering them dysfunctional (Victorian E.O. Commission 1977). Most of the technical schools across Australia were phased out during the 1980s in the general move towards a less stratified system of secondary schooling, similar to the British move to comprehensive schools at the same time, along with the dawning realisation that the labour market was fundamentally changing and the jobs for which the schools had initially purported to prepare students were no longer available. While the demise of the boys technical schools was sometimes lamented by parents and the popular press, it seemed that no-one regretted the passing of the girls technical schools. At the same time, the 1980s saw a heightened consciousness of questions around women and paid work. At school girls were increasingly challenged to think in terms of future careers rather than a job to fill in the time between school and marriage. Training in domestic skills had become much less central to these new visions of woman.

Meanwhile the public high schools in the 1950s and 1960s were characteristically organised along the lines of 'streaming' or ability grouping. Entering students were given a range of tests and placed in classes according to the resulting scores. The usual labelling applied: A, B and so on. Even in schools which did not use letter grades to identify the different levels, students readily decoded the labelling system, immediately recognising the implications of ability level. As a new teacher in a Victorian high school at this time I vividly recall my experience of teaching a class known as 3JK – it was ranked as the lowest ability class in Year 9 at my school; eighth in a ranking of one to eight. The class was all boys, by default rather than by arrangement, and none of the boys who attempted to resist my earnest attempts to engage them in learning (of French – my subject, and a compulsory one for all Victorian secondary students at the time!) was still at school two years later. On turning 15 they left school and went straight into the workforce.

The vast majority of the government high schools in Australia were coeducational, although in many cases (such as the one mentioned above) some classes became single-sex by default in terms of subject choice. In the junior high school years this meant, for example, that the domestic science class was girls-only whereas the woodwork class was all boys. In the senior years there were observable gender divisions in the mainstream subject areas, with the maths/science classes having a majority of boys and the history and language classes having more girls. This situation, although reasonably common, did not arouse much comment or educational concern from parents, teachers or the students themselves. Writing of girls' schooling in the 1950s Lesley Johnson (1990) describes the typical experience as 'under gendered', by which she means that gender distinction may well have formed part of the unwritten curriculum but was so much taken for granted that girls themselves had no cause to reflect on this as a feature of their existence, much less as a reason to feel any sense of disadvantage.

Questions of gender equity

Academic attention to questions of gender in Australian schooling provision began in the 1970s with Martin's article on 'Sex differences in educational qualifications' (Martin 1972), which showed that by and large boys got a good deal more from their schooling than did girls. For example, boys achieved more highly in senior years, were more likely to win scholarships and competitions across a range of year levels, more often represented their school in sporting competition and, most fundamentally, were significantly more likely to complete secondary schooling than were girls. Not surprisingly then, boys went on to university in much larger numbers than did girls, right across the social spectrum – although, as noted above, the tradition of university attendance was much stronger among middle-class males than all other groups. Around the same time Roper (1971) had published research showing, among other things, that non-government sector boys schools charged much higher fees and were much better resourced than were private girls schools. Many of these features were soon to change.

In the second half of the twentieth century education entered the political agenda and the Australian federal government paid attention. With the influx of migrants from Southern and Eastern Europe, many of the public primary schools were over full and the Catholic system had become impossibly overcrowded. Through the 1950s and 1960s teachers were in short supply around the country. While education had hitherto been a responsibility of the state governments, it became clear that the states needed commonwealth assistance if the much-needed improvements in schooling were to happen. Federal government moves to remedy the situation operated across a range of fronts. One strategy was the institution of tertiary studentships, scholarships and bursaries to encourage more young people into teaching. These initiatives were enormously influential in assisting numbers of working-class women and men to gain entry to university and to undertake teaching as a career.

There was also the issue of federal funding directly to the schools. In the late 1950s, for the first time, federal money was directed into the formerly 'private' schools, initially to boost the nation's educational achievement in science (Dudley & Vidovich 1995, p. 58). The federal Liberal government of the time saw the need for improved levels of science education so that Australia could become a competitive player in the post-Sputnik era, a time that was characterised by a high degree of optimism in scientific progress. As a consequence of this worldview, science became an important subject in Australian schools in the second half of the twentieth century.

Increasingly then, science became seen as an area in which intellectual ability was particularly important and one in which 'bright' students did very well. Many of these students were boys. In the 1970s and 1980s several projects to enhance the position of girls and science were able to show a clear relationship between the ways in which school science was presented, the books and the teaching content that were geared to boys' interests, and a masculinised pedagogy involving a good deal of competition and harsh punishments for underperformance (Kelly 1981). One study showed that before the end of primary school, children's scientific interests were distinguishable along gender lines, with the boys opting for topics such as 'the insides of a battery' and the girls choosing 'how a baby grows inside its mother' as their most preferred area of scientific study (Dawson 1981). Of course this result does not indicate separate learning styles so much as the children choosing culturally sanctioned interests that are gender appropriate. The task for the teacher is to involve boys in biology and girls in electronics rather than simply leave them to their already formed choices.

In the early 1970s the Commonwealth Schools Commission was established, a move that signalled increased federal attention to educational issues. The reports of the Commonwealth Schools Commission, which identified particular problems within the existing educational provision, were to lead to the channelling of federal funds to larger sections of the previously independent school sector on the basis of demonstrable need. While the state governments were and continue to be the main source of funding for the public school sector, increasing amounts of federal funds were directed toward the non-government schools. This situation has continued to the present.

For the interests of this book, the intervention of the federal government into schools was significant as it gave legitimacy to the principle of equity as central to Australian educational provision. Equal opportunity in education became a key plank in governmental education policy, especially after the election of the federal Labor government in 1972. As never before, government, teachers, parents and the broader community expected improved educational provision and were alert to issues of inequity within the existing system. These moves set the scene for concerns about the issue of gender equity in education to be raised.

With the release of the Interim Committee report of the Commonwealth Schools Commission, *Girls, School and Society*, in 1975, girls were identified as constituting a particular area of disadvantage in Australian schooling. Coincident with the rise of what is often labelled 'second wave feminism', a spate of research began around the country into aspects of gender equity in education – all driven by the identification of girls as a disadvantaged group. These studies showed that girls were typically marginalised in schooling in terms of their length of school experience, their academic achievements, their patterns of subject enrolment, their opportunities for leadership and even in terms of their capacity to be known by their teachers and their school communities. Education departments responded by setting up positions associated with equal opportunity and in government schools around the country committees were put in place with the task of ensuring that the school operated in gender inclusive ways. Generally the role was taken up by female staff members who were widely understood to be 'taking care of the girls'.

There were several policy developments to emerge from this work. After a considerable number of conferences on girls and education in each of the states, all of which launched reports into girls and education, the Schools Commission produced the 1984 document *Girls and Tomorrow: The Challenge for Schools* which took up many of the issues first raised in *Girls, School and Society*. Following this *The National Policy for the Education of Girls in Australian Schools* was released in 1987, giving further indication of the seriousness with which the federal government approached gender equity in education. Education departments were instructed that every official report of schooling processes should be broken down by gender. Thus there were, for the first time in many cases, gender records of school attendance, subject enrolments, teacher numbers, achievement levels and so on. All reporting of schooling outcomes was almost always accompanied by a comment on gender inclusivity.

Another dimension to be addressed at the official policy level was the issue of sexual harassment in schools. Following the passage of the federal *Equal Opportunity Act* in 1984, sexual harassment policies and procedures had been established in most schools around the country – at least within the government school sector. Some of the non-government schools, especially the single-sex schools, were slower in this development, possibly being less aware of the need. The majority of Australian schools undertook to prepare students to participate in a society in which sexual harassment was illegal and perpetrators were answerable under the law. This meant making students aware of the issues – and of their rights – a wide-reaching campaign of public awareness with schooling leading a process of cultural change.

The National Policy for the Education of Girls in Australian Schools was followed in 1993 by a *National Action Plan for the Education of Girls in Australian Schools* (MCEETYA 1993), which offered detailed criteria for implementing programs designed to boost the educational achievements of girls. With the election of the Liberal government in 1996, the orientation changed and later that year the government released *Gender Equity: A Framework for Australian Schools* (MCEETYA 1996), a development clearly inspired by the increasing publicity given to the boys in education movement (Gill & Starr 2000). The current educational scene is one in which questions of gender equity continue to be matters of public controversy as well as strategic action.

Gender and school retention/enrolments

One of the most immediate consequences of the attention directed at girls' schooling was the change in gender distinction relating to school retention. In the early days of schooling in Australia boys were more likely to complete school than girls; this long-established pattern had continued up until the mid 1970s. However, following the publication of the Schools Commission report, *Girls, School and Society*, by the late 1970s the situation was reversed and girls as a group became more likely to complete school than boys, a situation that continues today. More girls now complete the years of secondary schooling and take the end of school examinations whereas boys are more likely to leave school before the senior years. Interestingly, the disparity in school completion between girls and boys continues despite reasonably steady increases in school retention rates as a whole. The latest report on the Longitudinal Surveys of Australian Youth (LSAY) reveals that, in the current population of 19-year-olds, 26 per cent of males left school before completion as compared with just 16 per cent of females, a much smaller proportion than fifteen years earlier when 62 per cent of males and 51 per cent of females had left school before completion (McMillan & Marks 2003). Comments about the problem of boys' early leaving must be seen against the broader picture in which it is clear that a much higher proportion of young Australians now completes schooling than at any earlier time.

Nor is it possible to presume from these figures that girls are favoured by the current system to the detriment of boys. A major study commissioned by the federal Department of Education, Training and Youth Affairs (Kenway et al. 2000) revealed that by age 24 young men were significantly more likely to be in full-time work or some form of education and training than were young women, a disproportion that continued with age. This finding was based on the fact that whereas most universities report a higher number of young women in their first-year enrolments, especially in the general humanities courses, teaching and nursing, more young men are enrolled in post-school education and training across a wider range of endeavours. What this study revealed is a picture of young Australians continuing to embark on gender distinct post-school career paths, with the possible exception of the minority enrolment in highly prestigious professional courses such as law and medicine, in which there is approximately equal representation of men and women undergraduates. However, the appearance of gender equity in these professional courses also appears somewhat of a chimera, considering the senior levels of both professions which continue as male strongholds. In attempting to understand why the post-school distinction exists, it is instructive as a first step to look at school subject enrolments.

In Australian secondary schooling, enrolments in the senior years continue to show pronounced gender distinction in student subject choices. This feature was first documented in the Schools Commission report of 1975 and has continued in the face of strenuous campaigns such as the one to encourage more girls into maths and science. Several features of the gendered enrolment patterns warrant noting here. First, there is a general tendency for boys' enrolments to concentrate on a narrow group of subjects, often involving elements of the maths and science stream, whereas girls' enrolments are more typically spread across a range of subjects. Reportedly some of the most vocal opposition to the press for more girls in science and maths came from teachers of history and languages who had reason to fear losing their best students as a result of this campaign. Subject choice in senior school has clear implications for post-school options in terms of apprenticeships and tertiary education requirements. Furthermore, the Tertiary Entrance Rank (TER), which determines entry to particular university courses, is calculated on the basis of success in senior school subjects. This structure of assessment also has gendered implications. One West Australian study (Peck & Trimmer 1994) showed that the same array of student marks resulted in very different gender profiles of success and hence tertiary admissions, depending on the number of subjects included in the aggregate rank score. When only the best three student marks were aggregated more boys ranked highly, but when all seven subjects were included there were very many more high-ranking girls. The study is particularly interesting in that it shows gender difference as an artefact of the educational treatment rather than emerging 'naturally' from the students themselves. Thus in situations of heightened specialisation one can expect a predominance of males, whereas females appear more often when assessments take account of a broader range of endeavours.

Boys' education – the 'new disadvantaged'?

The heightened gender consciousness that became a feature of Australian education in the late twentieth century was to lead, in a fashion similar to that in the United Kingdom and North America, to a concern focused on boys' education. In this view boys are seen as the 'new disadvantaged', their needs typically unmet and their schooling as preparing them only for imminent failure. Currently teachers' complaints about the behavioural problems of boys are a constant feature of news reports, of education conferences and in-service teacher professional development. There is no doubt that concern is warranted by the large numbers of boys leaving schooling without any formal qualification. However, it is also important to ask the question: Which boys? (Teese et al. 1995; Gilbert & Gilbert 1998). Certain boys continue to be the success stories of standard education, as revealed by merit listing and prizes for senior school leavers published annually in the popular press. Analysis reveals the fact that by and large the middle-class boys continue to be well served by their schooling experience, in contrast to working-class boys (Teese et al. 1995). Connell et al.'s thesis concerning the need to develop an education that is organic to working-class interests in Australia (as distinct from the present system which functions in ways organic to middle-class interests) identified the problem to come in the case of these boys (Connell et al. 1982). In this analysis the standard competitive academic curriculum was seen to serve the interests of the middle class but to constitute the working class as 'other', to be the losers in the competitive system which requires winners and losers. Elsewhere analysts have pointed to the demise of unskilled labouring jobs typically undertaken by boys who are now required to stay in a school system from which they are routinely alienated and classed as failures. Thus there are explanations from both within school and beyond school that attempt to account for the current problems in boys' education.

At the moment the emphasis placed by spokespersons for the boys' education lobby is not on the ways in which the system is failing some of the students, especially those from poorer backgrounds. Rather the finger is pointed at boys as a new form of essentialism – the problem is not with the system per se but rather with the ways in which fundamental male needs are not being met in the current school arrangements. As evident in the quote from the boys school principal earlier in this chapter, this insistence on seeing the problem as bound up with essential male needs rather than socially produced factors is then used to argue the case for boys-only schools, with the suggestion that coeducation limits boys' development and is antithetical to masculinity (Phillips 2002). Of course not all the proponents of boys-only schooling espouse the extremes of the position, but the notion of the specificity of male needs is certainly getting more airplay in current debates than ever before.

Summary

All of these features of Australian educational debates are involved in any discussion of the relative merits of single-sex as compared with coeducational schools. Issues of curriculum, of ability and how it is demonstrated, of subject choice, of academic outcomes, of psychological maturity among other things have been investigated in attempts to provide the definitive answer to the question: Which way to school? School leaders, former and current principals, administrators, teachers and school council chairs have also weighed into the debate, often from positions of great conviction in terms of their own particular experience. Many spokespersons cite their own educational experience as evidence for their particular position – a device that recalls the wisdom of the old Chinese proverb about never being able to step into the same river twice. In other words, because a process worked well once you can't assume the same set of issues will apply in any later revisiting of the experience. In a similar vein, the experience of attending a boys school in the 1960s is most probably very different from that afforded by going to that same school today. The following chapters will review the studies that have been conducted around the question of school gender context and set up a framework for addressing that question.

Firstly though, it is important to reiterate that in investigating schooling we are dealing with a social institution, one that has been constructed by people in particular ways and for particular reasons. Investigations into the functioning of schools cannot be compared with laboratory testing – the variations due to the diversity of human experience are too closely involved in every interpersonal encounter and they resist control or even quantification as variables. However, it is possible to say some sensible things about the question and hopefully gain new insights that can be applied to any particular set of local circumstances.

2

GIRLS AND EDUCATION: Gender enters the educational agenda

Overview

This chapter describes the movement from the mid 1970s to foreground issues of gender equity in Australian schools, which began with a focus on girls and learning. The initial press for single-sex schooling appeared as a feminist response to the ways in which schools were seen to have traditionally discriminated against girls. Subsequently educational theory moved away from seeing girls as victims and focused instead on the construction of gender in schooling. The agenda for educational reform became much more complex.

Writing of the gendered nature of social institutions, commentators have repeatedly observed the inevitable struggles involved when an institution which was originally reserved for one gender is required to accommodate the other. Debates around the opening of universities to women were immortalised by Virginia Woolf in the essay *A Room of One's Own* in which she referred to the issue of library privileges or permission to walk on the grass as symbolic of the larger proscription against women within the English university system in her time. In Australia, questions around women's position within the legal system, their access to seats in parliament and to certain exclusive clubs and sporting arenas have constituted ongoing debates throughout the twentieth century. Some vestiges of these struggles are still around today. Frequently these issues hinged on what would appear to be fairly trivial points, such as the need to outfit parliamentary buildings with appropriate numbers of women's toilets. At the same time, the very triviality of these oppositional stratagems suggests the long-standing, deeply held fears evoked by the proposed radical change of allowing women in. Little wonder then that educational institutions were marked with a similar degree of gender specificity and resistance when they were initially required to admit girls and women and then later, when they were forced to examine their operations in the interests of equal opportunity and inclusivity.

Staffing structures and why they matter

In thinking about gender and institutions it is noteworthy that social institutions that were originally seen as female only, such as the professions of nursing, of early childhood teaching, of aged care, did not appear to register the same degree of intransigence when it came to admitting men. And the men who did enter these non-traditional fields were frequently hailed as ground breakers, as marked for special treatment, and their rise through the ranks was often notably more rapid than that of their female counterparts. Such differences are of course able to be explained in terms of the gender differences in status and power associated with men's work and women's work. In view of Australia's highly gender segregated labour force it is perhaps less than surprising that there is now a good deal of difficulty in attracting more men into teaching, a field with lower pay and less status than other comparable graduate destinations. The connection between the valuing of teaching and a gender hierarchy in terms of status and power is undeniable: the younger the children involved, the more likely their education is to be seen as women's work and the consequent lower ranking of the career in terms of status and monetary reward.

From an early age Australian school children become aware of the school-based gender hierarchy and reliably presume, along with students in New Zealand and North America, that in schools men are principals and women are teachers (Strober & Tyack 1980; Smith 1985). The following extract comes from a qualitative investigation (Gill 1992a) into the ways in which upper primary children explain gender and institutional hierarchy. We were talking about the ways in which school staffing typically had male teachers in the upper years of primary school. The children had assured me that there was 'no sexism' at their school and that everybody was equal. However, they did comment most positively on their experience of male teachers:

Annie: Men teachers are good at making you work.
Lia: I felt more important at school when I got into
         a man's class.

And about the question of women as principals:

John: A man would probably run a school better ...
Luca: The kids would take advantage of her
          [a female principal] ...
Mark: A male principal would be better because women
          aren't into sport...

When asked why they thought it was usual to have women in the junior primary years and men in the senior classes and the principal's office they said:

Karen: Little kids are more used to their mothers at home and
          they are more likely to get on with a lady teacher ...
Briony: (with great assurance) Women like little kids better.
Eliza: Little children are scared of men ... it's something
          psychological ... they're taller ... some grow beards
          and that gets you a bit scared ... (Gill 1992a)

In other words, the children read the gender hierarchy of typical school staffing arrangements as fitting with a traditional gender schema of men in powerful positions and women doing the nurturing of the young. They are here constructing their understanding in terms of biologically determined attributes and positions in the school – the association of women and babies, or of beards and maleness and being somehow a bit frightening. Without having been explicitly taught, they interpret their environment along gendered power lines. Of course this analysis may not hold true for all young people and in many schools there are now women principals, at least in the primary division. However, the evidence cited above does suggest the ways in which young people build understanding of the workings of power in terms of their actual experience – which is part of the rationale for making schools more gender inclusive in terms of their staffing structures.

Curriculum and academic rigour

At this stage in the discussion of girls and education it is important to recall that schools were originally designed for boys only. The English Public Schools, most of which were elite academic institutions, were modelled on the great monastic traditions of the Middle Ages. Their brief was to educate boys in ways befitting their social position, their community being the wealthy middle class whose numbers had vastly increased by the nineteenth century. These schools served as a model for the traditional private schools in Australia. Like them, the Australian schools were single-sex institutions that offered rigorous academic curriculum along with competitive sports – the cult of the healthy mind and the healthy body famously adopted by Headmaster Arnold at Rugby in nineteenth-century England. Boys educated at these schools became leaders in their professions and the wider Australian community – throughout the twentieth century significant numbers of their graduates became federal and state parliamentarians (Encel 1970). In each of the Australian states, schools of this type were established early in the colonial era and some continue today.

Few of the private girls schools initially offered the degree of academic rigour that was typical of the boys schools. Most of these institutions provided a curriculum of languages, music and 'polite accomplishments' seen as befitting the needs of the wealthy young women who were their students. Research in the late 1970s provides the comment that: 'Until very recently most of these schools took as their main task the production of a femininity which complemented the masculinity dominant in the class milieu' (Connell et al. 1982, p. 96). Not until the second half of the twentieth century did this regime undergo significant change when the wealthy client community began to review its ideas about the educational needs of their daughters. As Connell noted, it was the demand from middle-class parents for an academic education for their daughters which fuelled the 'academic turn' in the private girls schools and impelled them to broaden their curriculum offerings to include mainstream academic subjects and aim for university entrance (Connell et al. 1982). In a somewhat ironic inversion of the relation between traditional girls' schooling and social privilege, Connell found that parents whose wealth was derived from business were particularly interested in their daughters obtaining professional qualifications because they didn't think business would 'wear' the idea of a woman in management.

Rethinking the nature and purpose of schools

The project of making girls' education more comparable to that of boys was not simply a question of offering the same subjects for study – although obviously this move constituted an important element in the process. Of course cultural change cannot be brought about so easily. What was required was a general re-thinking about what schools were for and how they functioned. At the same time educationists needed to be aware of the changes relating to gender positions in the wider society for which their students were destined. The second half of the twentieth century was to prove to be turbulent times for Australian education in this regard.

As noted in the previous chapter, interest in the education of girls in Australia began in the early 1970s and took off at a great rate from then. By this stage, as a result of the federal government's initiative of offering teaching studentships and scholarships to alleviate the acute school staffing shortages, there were large numbers of young women undertaking university courses and then finding their way into teaching. Primary teaching had long been accepted as one of the few career choices available to Australian women, although until the 1970s they were required to resign on marriage[1] and were paid significantly less than their male counterparts. Despite these career disincentives, for much of the last century women outnumbered men in the primary division, although not in leadership positions. In South Australia in 1979, for example, women made up 68 per cent of all primary school teachers but only 10 per cent of primary school principals and at secondary level women accounted for 43 per cent of all teachers but only 9 per cent of principals (Keeves 1982).

To some degree this situation can be explained by the compulsory resignation of women on marriage, hence most women teachers lacked the seniority to become principals. Even after the marriage bar was lifted, the propensity of women to have career breaks for child bearing meant that numbers of women at the senior levels were slow to materialise, although the current situation appears much improved. There are ongoing analyses which claim that the traditional image of the school principal continues to be of a man in charge, such that the role of principal is constructed as masculine, a feature which can produce particular sets of problems for women who undertake that role (Starr 1999).

The majority of school teachers are women, and the proportion of female teachers increased steadily over the twenty years to 2002. In full-time equivalent terms, there were 2.1 female teachers for every male teacher in 2002, up from 1.4 in 1982. The female/male ratio was most pronounced at the primary school level where there were 3.8 female teachers for every male teacher in 2002, increasing from 2.4 in 1982. The gender balance was more equal at the secondary school level, with 1.2 female teachers for every male teacher in 2002, up from 0.8 in 1982.

Source: Schools, Australia, ABS cat. no. 4221.0.

The situation with regard to high schools was different: secondary teaching, traditionally connected to university education, had established itself as a male domain and continued to have a majority of men teachers through the last century. However, from the 1970s the numbers of women teachers in secondary schools around the country greatly increased because of the combined effects of the scholarships program and the expansion of the high school system to cope with the dramatic increase in numbers of students. The increase in student numbers had come about as a result of the government's immigration policy, as well as the 'baby boom' post World War II and increasing parental expectations that children would complete secondary school. The young women who entered teaching were often the first generation in their families to attend university. Many were readily recruited as activists in the girls and education movements that took off around the country after the publication in the mid 1970s of *Girls, School and Society*. The gender issue that Johnson had noted as 'underdone' in the 1950s was by the late 1970s in full swing. Gender awareness – or as it was then termed 'women's consciousness raising' – was everywhere, especially in activist feminist teaching circles.

The girls and education movement investigated

The two dimensions inevitably addressed in discussions of equity in education revolve around questions of access and questions of outcomes. Up until the mid twentieth century the majority of Australian girls did not have access to education past the compulsory years. Secondary schooling was not widely available within the government system. As a general rule only wealthy families could afford to send their children to fee-paying schools. In addition, the fact that parents were apparently more likely to be willing to pay for their sons' than their daughters' education (Roper 1971), coupled with the insufficient supply of high school places, had meant that most girls did not get the chance to finish high school.

Once the state governments saw fit to make significant commitments to the provision of secondary schools around the country it might have been imagined that girls and young women would have been equally able to study at higher levels as boys and young men. However, some blocks to girls' education remained. The first was both familial and cultural. Parents, it seemed, were still more inclined to support sons in education than daughters. Boys were encouraged to remain at school in the interests of improving their job prospects while girls were understood as being less interested in career and earnings.

More disturbingly perhaps, these views were also prevalent in the schools, with teachers expecting more of boys than girls (Bernard 1979; Evans 1979). And schools were then – even as they are today – largely shaped by prevailing cultural norms. Rather than being an agent of social transformation, Australian schooling in the 1950s and 1960s was seen to work to confirm girls and boys as different species with very distinct attributes and capacities. The stark contrast in enrolment patterns in senior schooling at the time underscored the different pathways typically undertaken by young Australians after they left school.

While there have been significant improvements in school retention rates in recent times, especially for girls, the different patterns of enrolments persist.

Girls as disadvantaged in 'malestream' schools

During the 1970s several Australian research studies were able to replicate what had first been seen overseas, namely that the typical ways of schooling in Australian schools appeared to be modelled on the boys-only pattern. In other words, having girls in the classroom sitting alongside the boys did not necessarily alter the established male-governed ways in which schooling operated. Simply being in the same classroom as boys did not mean that girls' educational experiences were equal to those of boys. Not only were boys seen as taking up more of the classroom airspace, more likely to be reprimanded for bad behaviour and untidy work, they were also more likely to be given help in attaining literacy, more likely to be school captain, more involved with school extracurriculum and team sports, more often mentioned in school publications, more often called on in class and so on. The phenomenon that had been identified by Spender in her work in British schools (Spender 1980; Spender 1982), girls' invisibility in the classroom and public arena of schooling, was repeatedly identified as a feature of Australian schooling. Most particularly, attention was drawn to the boys' 'domination' of the single largest piece of standard school equipment – the oval. In schools around the country the large open playing area available in most Australian schools, both primary and secondary, was routinely colonised by one half of the school population. It was used and defended as boys' territory – as it had been from the very early days of schooling in this country. As Miller notes, writing of secondary schooling midway through the twentieth century:

At lunch and recess times, boys used the oval while girls were confined to the school grounds 'owing to the risk of injury'. Even for sport the girls were allowed to use the oval for one and a half afternoons per week. (Miller 1986, pp. 143–4)

While other aspects of gender distinction in schooling practice had been noted in research from the United Kingdom and North America, it was this business about the oval that became a salient feature of gender inequality in Australian schools and a target for research and redemptive action. Perhaps as a consequence of the ubiquitousness of the oval and its associated male-dominated games of football and cricket, perhaps because it constituted a clear case of one gender group possessing something the other didn't, perhaps because it was an issue that presented as remediable … the oval became an early site for direct action in the interests of girls.

For all of these reasons – and especially since many teachers were dismayed to realise that they had for so long accepted the oval as boys' territory – there began around the country a series of initiatives designed to remedy the situation. The most common strategy was to institute 'girls' day' on the oval, which meant designating one or two days per week on which no boys were permitted onto the oval. Not surprisingly, such strategies produced a good deal of angst and vociferous resistance, especially since the girls had not been accustomed to using the oval for their play and tended not to take up the privilege accorded them. Of course the awareness of one group's 'missing out' and needing 'special treatment' that was behind these efforts was not destined to produce girls as the strong, independent, self-aware, young women the feminist teachers were looking for. But it was a beginning.

At the same time the issues around the oval and its use provide a microcosm of many of the initiatives undertaken in the interests of offering more inclusive, more equal educational treatments to girls in schools. Similar struggles were encountered around the question of access to the computer room, to positions of officially sanctioned student power within the school such as class monitor, prefect or school captain, to being mentioned in school assemblies and newsletters, to speaking in class, to doing woodwork and playing brass instruments in the school band. In all of these areas teachers undertook strategies designed to redress the existing gender imbalance that had for so long gone unnoticed. Teacher education routinely included the message of gender equity, which was interpreted by at least some students at the time as being told 'not to forget about the girls'.

All too often the issue about gender during the 1970s and 1980s became understood as something to 'help the girls' – a way of thinking that carried with it particular traps. By constituting girls as the group needing help, as victims of current provision, feminist educators ran the danger of disempowering the very target of their efforts to create strength and self-sufficiency. Despite good intentions, many of the strategies did little to further the long-term interests of developing assured, confident young women. By the 1990s some feminist commentators were raising serious questions about the effects of such treatments and the thinking that underpinned them. In particular, Lyn Yates challenged the notion of 'girl friendly schooling' in terms of the approaches this orientation commended being not necessarily in the best interests of girls. By the mid nineties she was asking 'Who are girls and what are we doing to them in schools?' in a paper that reflected her concern that girls were being positioned as being intellectually fragile, as needing special help and as less than clear thinking, autonomous and effective young women (Yates 1996). While many of these concerns were aroused in terms of the general philosophies of education of girls, there were also particular curriculum concerns.

Curriculum matters

As a consequence of the research finding that girls were less likely to continue with the prestigious maths and science subjects than were boys, a number of schooling initiatives were undertaken to promote the idea that girls could and should do maths and science. The use of single-sex classes for these subjects was one such initiative and is discussed in a later chapter. In mainstream, coeducational, government schools several other initiatives took place. A well-funded widely publicised government program, 'Maths multiplies your chances' attempted to develop in girls and their parents the conviction that the study of mathematics was very important for girls in terms of careers and life choices generally. One regularly televised image used to promote this campaign consisted of an unhappy girl locked into a cage, her restriction being apparently a direct result of her lack of mathematical knowledge. In-service professional development for teachers involved courses on the teaching of maths 'for girls' and several leading international scholars toured the country giving lectures based around the theme of 'Girls can! … do maths' and/or attacking the idea that 'Real girls don't do maths' (Willis 1989). Meanwhile many mathematics teachers, both male and female, were seen as particularly effective if their female students achieved success, while teachers in other subject areas were openly resentful of the campaign as they felt they were being robbed of their best students – bright girls who would traditionally have been doing history or classics but were now being lured into mathematics.

At the same time there were oppositional movements among feminist teachers too. The focus on mathematics was criticised as promoting one area of learning – and one with traditionally masculine overtones in terms of enrolment patterns and teaching principles and practices – above other areas which were seen as more female friendly, less overwritten with masculine values and approaches. Citing Audre Lorde's maxim about the impossibility of dismantling the father's house with the father's tools (Lorde 1984), some feminist teachers openly resisted the press for mathematics and science for girls in schools. Consequently, there were efforts to reclaim the curriculum for the humanities subjects as more female appropriate in line with the idea of 'girl friendly' schooling. At least one government girls school opted out of the maths curriculum altogether and initiated a different set of study practices that included computer skills but which effectively precluded any of its students from undertaking the public examinations in mathematics. This development is important in that it registers a change from a pro-girl position based on the claim for girls to get the same opportunities as boys (the classic equity of access argument) to one that was prepared to challenge the rightness of what had been considered, until that time, the hallmark of a good education. The maths/science domination of an unwritten, although sometimes explicit, curriculum hierarchy was in contention.

Linked to the issues around girls and maths/science education was the press to encourage girls into 'non-traditional' careers which were directed towards girls gaining apprenticeships in manual crafts such as carpentry, metalwork and so on. For a relatively short time in the 1980s this initiative gained momentum. Publications such as Foster's (1984) *Changing Choices* and Towns' (1985) *The Responsibility to Educate Girls for a Technologically Oriented Society* were evidence of educational strategies to broaden girls' career options. However, changes in the labour market and the accompanying downturn in this sort of work meant the initiative was short lived. Interestingly, it was one strategy that provoked resistance from girls themselves. From a 1988 interview with a group of Year 10 girls who were talking about curriculum offerings at their girls school comes the following excerpt:

> Annie (conspiratorially): This school's trying to turn us into
> macho women!!!

Int: What are macho women?
Katy: Yeah ... you know ... everything's 'non-traditional' and that ...
Pria: Yeah, they want us to be boilermakers and plumbers ... ugh!
Int: Are you saying you don't want to think about those sorts of jobs?
Selma: Nah ... we don't want them ... we just wanna have fun!

At which stage the group burst into a spontaneous rendition of 'Girls just wanna have fun ...' amid much giggling. (Gill 1992a)

These girls, along with many of their peers, were claiming the right to adopt a fairly traditional style of femininity in the face of their teachers' urgings to realign their futures in terms of a more gender-neutral world. The situation is reminiscent of Bronwyn Davies' research with preschool children who rejected the self-consciously feminist storyline of *The Paper Bag Princess* in favour of more traditional accounts of the fairy tale world in which princes are always brave and handsome and princesses are usually the ones in need of being rescued (Davies 1989). It seems that traditional gender lines – which construct desire along with accepted modes of behaviour – are learnt from an early age and are often staunchly resistant to contrary messages. While some commentators have interpreted this phenomenon as evidence for biological determinism (the view that one's personality, likes and dislikes are determined by sex), a more powerful explanation comes from the understanding that young people pick up and engage with the language and storylines – the discursive practices – with which they are surrounded, and construct their self-understandings accordingly.

Current educational movements along the lines of 'critical literacy' are needed if schooling is to work beyond the gendered constraints of much of popular culture, which continues to recycle unnecessarily limiting and outdated storylines. In this connection it is interesting to speculate on the effects of some of the current elements in popular culture which do present young women as active, playful and less gender restricted and determined than those of previous media representations. Pippi Longstocking and Jo March find echoes in Buffy the Vampire Slayer in their portrayals of individualistic, powerful young women who make choices about their lives. It still seems unlikely, however, that large numbers of young women will be ready to be recruited into manual trades.

School retention

The situation around school retention is a different story, and one in which the official line regarding the value of school completion for girls was more successful. Up until the mid 1970s boys were much more likely to complete twelve years of schooling than were girls, a situation that reflected attitudes in the broader culture about the value of education for males and females. Until this time, boys were seen as more successful students – largely because many more of them completed schooling and gained university entrance (Martin 1972). The recognition of this disparity in school attendance and the consequent encouragement for girls to stay in education had an immediate and dramatic effect. By the late 1970s Australian girls as a group had become more likely to complete schooling than their male peers, a situation that prevails today both in Australia and the United Kingdom. This is not to suggest, however, that girls are now more effectively served by educational provision. In the early 1980s an analysis of the different educational pathways post school had shown that the boys who left school before completion frequently went into apprenticeships – the vast majority of which were unavailable to girls – and by age 19 there were significantly more young men than young women in some form of further education (Praetz 1983). A more recent large-scale federally funded study revealed that, although by the early twenty-first century there are more women in higher education than men, mostly in the areas of education and nursing, the gender pathways still exist. By age 24 young men are more likely to be in some form of education than young women, with consequent implications for earning power, career success, status and recognition (Kenway et al. 2000). The recent Longitudinal Surveys of Australian Youth (LSAY) report, based on the responses of some 13 000 young Australians who were in Year 9 in 1995, reveals similar gendered patterns of school leaving and entering the world of work (McMillan & Marks 2003).

What these findings underscore is the continuing importance of schooling for young women. For many more young women than young men, schooling constitutes the last engagement with formal education. Moreover, if girls leave school early they are at much greater risk than boys of never finding full-time work (Collins 2000). An Australian Council for Educational Research (ACER) study concluded:

> It may well be that completing Year 12 opens up a proportionately wider range of job possibilities for young women than for young men since most of the job market is open to men in any case. (Ainley & MacKenzie 1999, p. 113)

This comment indicates the different labour market positions available to young men and women in respect of their years of schooling. In other words it is much more important for girls to finish school than it is for boys, given their different positions in terms of employment prospects. For girls, early leaving positions them with a very poor chance of employment, whereas the early leaving boys have a distinctly higher chance of finding work. More girls do finish school but their employment possibilities are still weaker than those of boys who have left school without finishing. Kenway commented on the paradox that for girls 'schooling does not pay off as well as it might in career terms, yet they are very dependent upon it' (Kenway 2000, p. 75). While it is clearly desirable for all students to complete their secondary education, it is significantly more important for girls to do so in terms of the consequent effects of early leaving on their life chances.

While there are some encouraging signs of attention being given to re-entry schools and adults are increasingly encouraged to return to education, to complete schooling or to engage with subjects not previously studied, such programs reach only a very small section of the population. Schooling continues to be singularly important in shaping the attitudes to learning of the general population and it continues to be the last educational chance for large proportions of young women.

Girls and self-esteem

One feature of gender difference that was identified quite early in educational research concerns the difference in levels of self-esteem in favour of boys. It seems that boys in Australian schools, from as early as Year 5, consistently score more highly on standard measures of self-esteem than do girls. These measures involve responses to statements about being happy with one's appearance, feeling sure of one's ability in a range of tasks, both intellectual and physical, and being convinced that others have a similarly high opinion of oneself (Smith 1975). Gender difference along the dimension of self-esteem as measured by such means appears to be an enduring feature of the local school community.

From a psychological viewpoint, such results are not surprising, given the greater valorisation of maleness and male attributes in the wider society. Studies reliably report that many more girls express an interest in being a boy and playing with boy things than the reverse. Consequently, the differences in self-esteem could be read as young people's accurate perception of social values rather than as an internalised predisposition to inferiority. Notwithstanding the possibility of such a counter reading, the question of self-esteem was taken up by feminist educators as indicative of the lesser valuing of girls in the education system. Indeed, the lower measured self-esteem of girls accorded with studies of confidence levels in expectations of success and failure, fear of success and a body of psychological literature all reliably indicative of enduring gender difference.[2]

As a result, an array of curriculum projects designed to build self-esteem became available, especially in the primary schools, in the mid to late 1980s, and continued into the 1990s. Although well intended, many of these projects appear to have relied on variously contrived affirmations of self-worth – for example, 'Everyone in the group must say something nice about one other person!' – rather than well-theorised treatments. Consequently, it would appear unlikely that they would have a lasting effect. Research evidence is fairly clear in demonstrating that the most effective way to boost self-esteem is to experience success in one field or another. Children who have been successful at, say, maths or reading or tennis will have a higher self-esteem than those who haven't had that experience and they will be more likely to continue with the particular field of study.

The self-esteem movement appeared to peak in the late 1980s and then to peter out, although the term self-esteem has permeated the language of educators who tend to invoke it in their analyses of student weaknesses, which, as noted above, quickly become self-fulfilling prophecies. For instance, if a student is failing and that is explained by 'low self-esteem' it seems unlikely that the problem will be rectified. In order to build self-esteem the student requires successful learning experiences – in other words the cycle of failure must be broken. From the point of view of girls and education, the self-esteem explanation emerges as somewhat of a blind alley in an essentially circular argument.

The self-esteem argument has also been connected to the issue of single-sex schooling compared with coeducation. Phillips' early work (1980) had shown that girls in girls schools tended to have higher self-esteem than those in coeducational schools. However, the social class differences which have also been shown to affect levels of self-esteem are implicated here. The girls schools in this study comprised elite, non-government sector schools and to compare the girls' results with those of girls from low socioeconomic government coeducational schools is to fall into the trap of assuming gender context is the single relevant variable, a highly unlikely proposition.

Girls' 'preferred learning styles' – a red herring

One of the most persistent ideas to have emerged from the activity around girls' education was the notion of girls having 'learning styles' that were essentially and inevitably different from those of boys. This tendency to assume fundamental sex differences continues to be seen as intuitively reasonable by large numbers of teachers, and the idea was taken up vigorously by people taking the position of girls having 'special needs' in education. An immediate problem with the concept is that the idea of a special or different 'learning style' is readily understood as meaning different capacity to learn, different cognitive abilities, different biologically determined levels of intellectual functioning. Indeed the early studies in psychology had simply assumed that male and female brains were wired differently. Consequently, the majority of early psychological testing was based on the responses of male subjects as the primary model of brain. When girls and women were included, the intention appeared to be to demonstrate their peculiarity and lack of consistency.

By the mid 1970s a good deal of psychological research had established the fact that cognitive differences between males and females were both small and inconsistent over time, so much so as to warrant great caution in publicising their existence. Such was the conclusion from researchers on both sides of the Atlantic who had completed major overviews of all the existing work on this topic (Fairweather 1976; Maccoby & Jacklin 1976). These conclusions have subsequently been confirmed by further research which investigated the results of a large number of studies of sex differences in mental performance (Willingham et al. 1997). Thus there is a large body of established research that discredits the idea of innate sex difference in intellectual functioning.

In Australia, the volume of research in educational psychology was not sufficient to warrant similarly rigorous overviews, but the general results appeared to hold. In particular, Fairweather's finding that the younger the population tested, the less likely were any differences to be found, would appear to remove any grounds for essential difference in the ways in which males and females engaged in intellectual processing. Moreover, comparisons across a thirty-year span showed that differences that once existed appeared to diminish, indicating they were not caused by innate difference but rather through cultural conditioning. Rogers cites Feingold's study (Feingold 1988) of sex differences in scholastic aptitude which were seen to have declined 'precipitously' between 1947 and 1983, a finding she interprets to mean that the differences originally found reflected the degree of gender difference in the wider culture, a feature that had significantly narrowed by the 1980s. Similarly another study (Hyde et al. 1990) noted that gender differences in mathematics performance diminished dramatically post 1974 when compared with earlier studies. According to Rogers:

> This [the diminution of gender difference] is probably due to the changing attitudes about which careers are more appropriate for girls and which are more appropriate for boys. (Rogers 1999, p. 36)

From a purely cognitive perspective it seems that boys and girls go about the work of learning in similar ways, just as do people from different cultures and different age brackets. At the same time, from the indications above, what they learn and how quickly the learning progresses may well be influenced by the particular period and culture. For instance, young people in urban Australia currently appear to have untold skills in programming VCRs whereas older people in their households are significantly more tentative. Some cognitive theorists have consistently argued that the sorts of play experiences different children have may prepare them differently for later learning (Block 1984). For example, a child from the nineteenth century may appear to have been much more oriented towards playing with fairly primitive toys such as hoops and dolls and would probably be quite confounded if confronted with a Game Boy. This difference does not indicate that modern children are basically 'brighter' than their great-grandparent generation, just that the context is different. And, in present day society, boys as a group may score at a lower level on tests of literacy than do girls. This result does not indicate fundamental intellectual difference but rather that the skills involved may be less practised in boys' preschool and school activities than in those of girls.

Even more importantly, in every case of gender differences in intellectual functioning, such as the literacy one reported above, the degree of overlap is much greater than the degree of difference. This means that boys and girls taken as a group are more like one another than are all the boys or all the girls taken separately. While the overall score for girls on literacy achievement may be ahead of that of boys, these averages mask the fact that there will be many boys who score highly on this dimension and are indeed better than a good many girls. Thus it is unwise for teachers to accept notions that generalise in terms of gender differences in cognition as in every classroom there will most likely be some students on any dimension who are better than some others of the opposite sex. However, the environments in which people have been prepared to learn or prefer to learn may be rather different. The 'cultural baggage' that children bring to school is implicated in everything they do there, most particularly in their learning.

In other words, the finding of minimal gender differences in cognitive functioning does not discredit the volume of teachers' observations that account for differences in the ways in which boys and girls approached intellectual tasks. Young people are socialised into their gender positioning and they play out the results in a range of attributes such that, for example, many boys often respond positively to the idea of competition whereas many girls may feel threatened by it. In our culture at the moment, many girls may try harder with a bit of collaborative encouragement while for many boys it will possibly be an individual competitive achievement that draws the greatest effort. These effects are not produced by essential difference between the sexes but rather are learnt responses from the abundance of cultural messages through which young people learn to be girls and boys in our culture. They are not biologically driven innate characteristics, despite the enduring popularity of the Mars/Venus thesis. And there are many young people who don't conform – girls who love competition and boys who prefer to be team players, precisely because it is not written in their genes to be one way or the other.

However, there can be no doubt that the 'difference' thesis is attractive to many people in that it does readily explain so much and, in so doing, it removes responsibility from teachers. The implication that the learning style is already pre-set means that there is little to be done about it. The fact that such a pre-ordained function has the power to effectively negate the possibility of teaching for equity does not discourage some of the most passionate equity proponents from engaging with it, even though of course it should.

In acknowledging the potential effects of the environment on children's approaches to learning it is important to consider gender context as a particular feature of the environment. Do boys and girls learn more effectively in same-sex groups or in mixed groups? In an article written some fifteen years after the major study reported above, Eleanor Maccoby maintained her position that behavioural difference between males and females is minimal when considering individual test results. However, she also noted that gender differences in behaviours did emerge when young people were observed in social situations and that these differences varied in terms of the gender composition of the group (Maccoby 1990). This observation is important when considering gender and schooling. At the same time it is yet another demonstration of the fact that the differences noted do not emerge from the innate psyches involved but rather are produced by the situation in which the young people find themselves. Hence it is logical to suggest that their reactions will be coloured by the degree of gender typing typical of that cultural context and will vary in other situations. In a similar way sex-segregated schooling may be most appropriate in societies with rigid gender distinctions, but less so in more gender inclusive societies.

Gender and moral development

Gilligan's much cited thesis concerning gender differences in the ways in which young people approach moral questions is relevant here (Gilligan 1982). Her research challenged Kohlberg's thesis (Kohlberg 1981) about the moral development of children in which he showed that boys more typically achieved the higher levels of moral development whereas girls did not reach these high stages but tended to cluster around the middle. Having presented evidence for her case that gender socialisation typically predisposes young people to adopt different approaches to moral questionsg, Gilligan was able to show that the terms of Kohlberg's questions played to culturally induced male-appropriate thought patterns rather than female-appropriate ones. Thus boys were oriented to think in terms of the abstract principles involved, whereas girls tended to want to think about the personal and interpersonal responses of the actors. Importantly, Gilligan included evidence to the effect that girls could be taught to regard the question in terms of the underlying abstract principles and boys could be taught to take account of personal involvements (Gilligan 1982). It is unfortunate that the difference thesis arising from this work is much more often cited than its corollary, which positions the teacher as centrally important in recognising and transcending typical gender limitations. The temptation to see gender as fundamentally related to a pre-given set of attributes and related social practices is extraordinarily powerful. Such a vision can also be anti-educational in that it confirms individuals in limited positions and resists the possibility of full intellectual development.

Role models

Another term that recurs in discussions of gender equity and schooling treatments is 'role model', a term originating in Albert Bandura's psychology of social cognition (Bandura 1986), which stresses the part played by imitation as an important means of learning. Role-model theory accounts for the perceptible delight that small children find in playing with toy versions of adult implements such as lawn mowers, stoves, tea sets, prams and even ironing boards. In doing this they are copying behaviours associated with more powerful people in their life worlds such as their parents, carers or other adults. Note that they are not copying the person so much as the things they do, and achieving a sense of adult importance as a consequence. While the toys associated with these events are often distributed on a same-sex basis – it is rare for boys to be given ironing boards although they have been known to engage in play involving them – same-sex modelling is not an essential feature of this learning. A cursory visit to the toy store will demonstrate that the majority of dolls are given to girls and train sets and adventure games to boys. However, young children can and do interchange fairly readily in terms of gender-appropriate toys. They have even been known to engage in protracted argument about who will play the all-powerful Mummy! They happily model their behaviour on the significant adult in their circle. In this they are 'trying out' activities that are connected with a sense of power and purpose.

When the term role model is translated into current schooling arguments around gender it seems all too often to be assumed – if not explicitly stated – that it is desirable for young people to have same-sex 'role models'. Much of the argument put forward by the girls' education lobby concerned the need for girls to have 'same-sex role models' such as women science teachers, women principals and so on, so that the girls could not merely imitate the behaviours associated with the roles but in fact *identify* with them and model their futures around being such people. This notion derives from Freudian psychoanalytic theory, with its emphasis on same-sex identification seen as necessary for healthy gender identity development, and thus belongs with concepts such as the Oedipal crisis, penis envy and other fanciful ideas whose relevance to present social arrangements is decidedly problematic. In general, this theory can be seen to have been more appropriate in a world in which gender identity is clearly demarcated and reflects the very rigid sex-role stereotyping of the nineteenth century at the time of its origin.

During the 1970s and 1980s, when the girls' education movement gathered force, the gender imbalances between males and females in senior positions (for example, as principals or as teachers of high status maths/science subjects) constituted a striking feature of Australian educational arrangements. This situation precisely reflected the existing power distribution in the world beyond school. Not surprisingly then, the distribution of power within the schools was challenged in the interest of modelling a more equitable arrangement.

Superficially similar arguments are currently being vigorously recycled by the boys' education lobby in the claim that schools have become overly feminised and that there is an urgent need for more male teachers at all levels. While these arguments will be addressed in a subsequent chapter, suffice it to say that, in this case, the relatively low numbers of males in the teaching force and the increasing numbers of women in senior positions is not reflected in the hierarchical arrangements of the wider world such as those in government or private business where traditional gender distinctions still apply.

Now it seems perfectly reasonable to press for educational institutions to have equal numbers of women and men in positions of power and authority so that the young people in their care develop a gender inclusive awareness of how organisations work. However, this is not the same thing as arguing that such an arrangement is necessary so that the people in senior positions can serve as models. As anyone who spends time with young people is aware, they are prone to changes in fashion and scene – the latest fad is taken up very quickly – but only very, very rarely, if at all, are their present or future plans modelled around their teachers. Today's adolescents may rate the gear and general deportment of, say, Christina Aguilera or Eminem or Kasey Chambers, and they may copy their style of dress and tastes – and even life course – but they are much less likely to model themselves on Ms Smith in Science or Mr Brown in English. The point is that the role-model argument is one example of the ways in which gender issues have been taken up in the broader community and the media, but the logic of its adoption relies on a misunderstanding of how role theory works. Proponents of gender equity would do much better to ground their argument on the fairness and educational value of equal representation, a position which offers a much more solid basis for having women and men in positions of power.

Both boys and girls need to see women and men in positions of power and authority in their educational institutions. They need to learn to relate to men and women in these positions as they will likely graduate into a public world much less gender divided than before. It is probable that many boys will be in work situations with women bosses and girls may themselves become senior figures in institutions – the necessary learning involved operates both ways. Thus the equity argument applies to both sexes and should not be reduced to a gender politics that privileges one set of needs over the other. Nor should it be limited to arguing the virtue of same-sex schooling. Indeed it may be even more important for boys in boys schools to interact with women in senior positions because of their relative rarity in these environments. A similar argument could be made for girls in girls schools, even though the perception of men in senior positions is less of a rarity as the traditional gender order remains in many institutions in the world beyond school.

A more sophisticated argument

During the 1990s educational theorists became increasingly concerned with the problem of the representation of girls as victims, as deficit models, as lacking in intellectual rigour, as passive onlookers. Realising that this style of approach was seriously limited in what it could achieve for girls, researchers became interested in the ways in which language works to associate gender and social power – 'a real boy', 'only a housewife', 'woman driver' and so on. This approach, known as discourse theory, alerts researchers to the fact that language is not simply a transparent means of conveying the meaning of words, but that it also transmits whole systems of understanding around power. This orientation led into analyses of the ways in which gender positions, masculinity and femininity, were discursively produced in schooling practice. Such analyses offered much more powerful explanations for the widespread adoption of familiar gender positions than had the earlier 'victim' thesis. Researchers were able to show the subtle and nuanced ways in which the construction of gender operated in terms of versions of both masculinity and femininity, some dominant, others more marginal. Most importantly, they identified the barrage of gender positioning made available through daily school interactions among peers, among teachers and students, between students and texts and so on. Rather than seeing gender as something that was 'done to' young people to cause them to conform, it now became clear that young people are actively engaged in constructing their gendered selves in terms of the opportunities made available through schooling.

A powerful outcome of these analyses was to allow and encourage teachers to see the ways in which particular schooling practices, in which they and the students were involved, gave rise to gender distinction in behaviour and outcomes. These perceptions were to prove a much sounder basis for changing behaviours than the 'girls as victim' orientation had done. The importance of 'reflective practice' in teaching and teacher education was made manifest by these arguments. Teachers were encouraged to be consciously aware of the impact of their practice on their students and to be alert to the ways in which gender assumptions entered into their teaching. They were also encouraged to make explicit the gendered assumptions of students and make these attitudes and values part of the material for discussion in classrooms.

Summary

By the early 1990s the situation in Australian schools regarding gender was one of heightened awareness of the situation of girls. This is not to say that the issues around girls' education were taken up equally at all levels of education. Nor did it mean that the problems girls encountered in schooling had been resolved. Consistent and protracted research continued to reveal girls as a group as disadvantaged in terms of educational treatments and outcomes (Milligan & Thomson 1992; Collins et al. 1996). However, the work of the previous two decades had borne fruit in terms of the various national policies, the wider awareness of the issues and the adoption of practices associated with national strategies and action plans. While the initial strategies adopted in the interests of assisting girls' educational achievement were generally designed with the idea of counteracting girls' educational disadvantage, these were followed by movements to promote girls' achievements and visibility as participants in school and beyond. The focus moved from one of rendering girls' education more similar to that of boys through to one of recognising the specific achievements of girls, their ongoing participation in schooling and broadening their post-school possibilities. Instead of demanding that girls should have whatever was available to boys (a move that kept boys as the benchmark) the reformers were increasingly drawn to look at the ways in which education might be re-envisioned to encompass a more appropriate experience for girls, foregrounding girls' needs, hopes and desires. Throughout this period (1975–1990) there had existed a widespread, albeit unspoken, understanding that 'gender meant girls'. This situation was soon to change.

3

BOYS' EDUCATION: Questions of fact and rhetoric

Overview

This chapter begins by identifying the ways in which boys had been traditionally served by educational systems and proceeds to note some significant social and educational changes in the 1980s and 1990s, which continue to impact on the ways in which schooling is viewed and the successes and failures associated with it. Concerns with boys' education have led to some suggestions that boys need boys-only schools.

As we have seen in the previous chapter, up until around 1970 discussions of Australian education were mainly silent about gender. At the beginnings of the concern about girls and education there were no voices raised about matters to do with boys. Instead there appears to have been a general assumption that boys were the beneficiaries of a schooling system designed to suit their needs.

In this chapter I will demonstrate that, although some boys were well served by Australian schooling in that they achieved well in school, completed all twelve years and went on to university studies to gain entry to a profession, this was not true for the majority of young men. As McCalman has noted, the examination system which operated in Victoria in the first half of the twentieth century effected a rigorous sorting and sifting such that only those few young people deemed 'highly able' completed schooling and went on to further study (McCalman 1993). Analysis of education systems in the other states shows that this was the general pattern of educational experience in Australia. Writing of the situation in New South Wales, Teese notes:

Of every 100 pupils entering public secondary schools in New South Wales in 1948, one-fifth had departed by the second year, over half by the third year, 87 per cent by the fourth year and 90 per cent by the fifth year. (Teese 2003, p. 3)

In fact, the situation for most of the last century was that the vast majority of young Australians, both male and female, did not complete twelve years of schooling. Even in the case of those whose parents wanted and could afford to support them through secondary school (and there were more boys in this category) the outcome was often a Fail at Year 10 or Year 11, which effectively precluded them from higher education. So long as the widespread perception was that university study was only intended for those very few highly able people, this situation did not arouse public outcry. Indeed it was accepted by and large as the majority view, gleaned from the systematically constructed understanding that the level of achievement obtained was a reliable indicator of 'natural' ability – a necessary quality to undertake the senior school years and further study.

In this way Australian education operated as a meritocracy in ways much more similar to its British counterpart than to the situation in North America where the completion of high school was more commonly expected. The student profile in Australian secondary schools up until the 1970s was typically that of a pyramid, a broad base in the junior high school years that thinned out dramatically to the select few at the top in the senior years. Different school systems showed marked differences in school retention, too. The non-government school profile was less marked by student attrition than the government schools, with the Catholic system operating midway between the other two. The position of the different systems in terms of school retention in the 1970s was summarised in the following table:

Table 1
Percentage of first-year students remaining to Year 12 by school type

Schools	%
Independent	86
Catholic	43
State	30

Source: Connell et al. (1982), *Making the Difference.*

Clearly the chances of completing school were much higher for the minority of students who attended non-government non-Catholic schools at this time. It would, however, be wrong to assume that the majority of young people saw themselves as educational failures. Just as girls who did not complete high school did not necessarily regard themselves as stupid or underprivileged, no more did boys whose school experience finished at Year 10. In both cases these were typical encounters with formal education in Australia for most of the twentieth century. Although the Great Depression years of the 1930s had led some middle-class parents to strive for better education for their offspring – to which end some of them went to great lengths to enable the school fees to be paid – this was not true for the majority. Indeed, the ready availability of jobs for school leavers, especially boys, from the mid 1940s meant that young people's life chances did not appear to have been marred by not completing school. The stigma attached to 'dropping out of school' was much more real for American youth than for young people in this country, or for that matter in Britain. Australian teachers in the 1960s were often greeted by the response from students: 'Doesn't matter if I don't pass this year, I'm going to get a job'. Opting for a working life, and the attendant adult status, was seen by young people at the time as an attractive alternative to remaining in school as a dependant. Many young people who had demonstrated the ability to remain at school and had passed the examinations still chose to leave school and join the workforce – often as not to the envy of their peers who stayed behind.

In the latter part of the twentieth century, the privations of the immediate post-war era were followed in the late sixties and early seventies by an unheralded level of optimism. Boosted by the ready supply of cheap labour produced by the government's immigration policies, Australian parents became more interested in securing futures for their sons and daughters that were consistent with the goals of an upwardly mobile social group. There was an upsurge of interest from the broader public in the idea of university education and the entry to professional careers afforded by the completion of a degree. The federal government's initiatives in education were in line with these developments.

In the last quarter of the twentieth century, two features were to have great impact on public attitudes to and experience of education in Australia. One was the opening up of the university system with the establishment of some twenty new universities and hence many more students, comprised of a majority of school leavers along with others from adult entry programs. With this development, university education ceased to be the preserve of the privileged few, already blessed by wealth or sometimes simply high ability, but rather became the expectation of a much broader section of the general public. Of course this development impacted on the style of education at universities, too. At this time, higher education began a process of change from an elite to a mass education system, a process which forms a background to many of the current debates around higher education. The second feature impacting on public attitudes concerned the changes in the senior school years in terms of subject range and examination procedures, driven by the larger student numbers at this level. Both of these developments took place against a background of pronounced change in the labour market, with the demise of manufacturing and manual labouring and the rise of jobs in service industries associated with the retail industry, hospitality and tourism. Such labour market changes had immediate implications for the relationship between schooling, credentialing and the gender dimensions of the Australian workforce.

The broadening of the university system

With the removal of university fees in 1972, higher education became theoretically more widely available. However, the actual uptake of places continued to reflect the connection between higher education and social privilege. Despite the increased number of places and the lessening of the financial cost for students, the sons and daughters of working-class Australians were seldom represented among the student body – a feature that was even more observable in the higher status older universities than the newer ones.

Table 2
Undergraduate course enrolments, socioeconomic status (SES) profile, South Australia, 1996

High SES (25% of population)		Medium SES (50% of population)		Low SES (25% of population)	
1986	1996	1986	1996	1986	1996
39.3%	41.2%	47.7%	43.8%	13%	15.1%

Source: Ramsay et al. (1998), *Higher Education Access and Equity*.

As is evident from the above table, the established pattern of university students being more likely to come from the middle and high SES backgrounds continued between 1986 and 1996, despite the provision of more university places during this period.

The situation regarding gender imbalance in student numbers in higher education changed much more dramatically. By the late 1980s, with the establishment of nursing as a tertiary study at university and the reconfiguration of the former teachers colleges into newly amalgamated universities, the traditional gender division within universities was over-turned. Women, always heavily represented among students in the fields of teaching and nursing, became the majority of first-year students. Hence the picture of gender division in educational treatments becomes more complex.

Since the mid 1970s, girls as a group have been more likely to complete school than their male peers, and by the late 1980s there were more women entering universities than men. This scenario could be interpreted as the education system favouring girls and women over men and boys – indeed such has been the case of some of the proponents of boys' special needs in education. However, the situation is more complex than these superficial responses imply. For instance, if nursing were removed from the range of university studies the proportion of male and female students would be much more equal. If education were removed as well, the traditional male dominance would re-emerge. What we have here then is evidence of different gender pathways through higher education, at the same time as a larger proportion of young Australians engage in it. The changes within the higher education sector were to have effects on the senior years of schooling as well.

Curriculum changes

The short-lived strategy of public support of free university education through the tax system, along with the greater acceptance of the idea of finishing high school and going on to further study, were significant factors in changing popular attitudes to education and schooling. Although retention rates (referring to the proportion of students entering school who remain to the senior years)[1] fluctuated fairly dramatically through the nineties after peaking in 1991–1992, when compared with the situation some fifteen years earlier it is clear that there is a trend for significantly more young people to remain in school for the senior years (McMillan & Marks 2003). This feature has implications for the senior school curriculum. Instead of simply sorting out who was able (and therefore university material) from who was not, the senior years of school have become a challenge for teachers to devise suitable educational experiences for a much wider range of student interests.

While curriculum at this level has continued as a pre-requisite for university for those students going on to further study, for those not intending to go on to university, the purpose of the senior high school years is less clear.

For the past two decades curriculum in the post-compulsory years has been under continual review around the country, as have examination procedures associated with it. Despite attempts to revamp the study requirements to suit the student body, senior high school curriculum is still, in the early years of the twenty-first century, governed by the conditions of tertiary entrance rather more clearly than other considerations. The recent developments to do with VET (Vocational Education and Training) in schools constitute the most dramatic change in curriculum in the post-compulsory years and have succeeded in blurring the distinction between school and further education. Increasingly school completion is less likely to be seen as an end in itself as it becomes more connected to post-school learning pathways. Many schools include VET subjects as part of the study program in the senior years, while a much smaller number of students undertake some elements of university study while still at school. In addition, changes in student numbers in senior school appear to have exacerbated some of the existing distinctions between schooling sectors.

In the non-government school sector the traditional curriculum continues to dominate student experience. In their publicity the elite schools are prone to present their senior school examinations results and thereby pride themselves – and attract future clients – on the basis of their students' achievements. The TER (Tertiary Entrance Rank) emerges as the gold standard enshrined in these results and the basis of inter-school comparisons, a feature which further underscores the university orientation of these schools. Some of them explicitly market their schools in terms of preparation for university – 'tertiary literacy' is identified as the key learning area in some of these environments, so widespread is the assumption that this sort of schooling will lead on to higher education. Government schools in middle-class areas similarly gear their programs and school counselling towards maximising the chance for high student achievement in terms of university entry. Meanwhile, in schools serving less wealthy communities, the struggle is to maintain student interest in a much broader range of curriculum offerings, the rationale for which is often less clear than for those connected to higher or further education.

Table 3
Range of university places and TER scores associated with them, South Australia, 2003

University	Course title	TER cut-off 2003
University of Adelaide	Bachelor of Commerce	91.80
	Bachelor of Engineering (Computer Systems)	85.40
	Bachelor of Media	80.05
	Bachelor of Science	65.05
University of South Australia	Bachelor of Journalism	92.70
	Bachelor of Commerce	78.95
	Bachelor of Science	70.40
	Bachelor Engineering (Computer Systems Engineering)	60.05
Flinders University	Bachelor of Laws and Legal Practice	95.05
	Bachelor of Engineering (Computer Engineering)	77.25
	Bachelor of Science	70.20
	Bachelor of Business Economics and Government	62.05

Source: Compiled from university prospectuses.

When the results of the senior school assessment are published, it is evident that some students, both boys and girls, perform at very high levels of achievement, while others produce less spectacular results. As shown in table 3, the expanded tertiary sector includes an array of course offerings with a broad range of entry scores. Currently there are sufficient tertiary places for roughly half the age cohort of school leavers. This is not to say, however, that all students are accepted into their first choice of course, but many more enrol at university than in previous times.

Changes in school retention rates

Coincidentally, with the removal of some academic and financial barriers to university study came significant change in the labour force. With the demise of the manufacturing industry and its need for manual labour, the ready appeal of school leaving, associated with picking up a job from a range of offerings, diminished markedly as such jobs became less and less available. For a certain period through the late 1980s this perception was associated with a boost in school retention as young people believed what they were told, that the higher the level of education achieved the more likely you were to find work. School retention in South Australia peaked at 91 per cent during this period. However, this time was short lived. In the face of the actual experience of not being able to find a full-time job, even if they had completed school, young people began again to vote with their feet. Retention rates, which had been increasing, dropped in the early 1990s in several states. Subsequently, they appear to have reverted to an upward trend that maintains the previous gender difference wherein girls are around 10 per cent more likely to complete school than boys. Overall the figures show a gradual rise in retention such that by 2002 approximately 84 per cent of girls and 74 per cent of boys completed secondary school (McMillan & Marks 2003). While the rates still vary with school sector and student background, with the non-government schools showing stronger retention than the government schools, the increase in school retention has been most marked in government sector students.

How these changes affected boys' education

The point of all this movement and change for the analysis of gender and schooling presented here is that these changes impacted more heavily on boys than girls. The boys who, once having failed to succeed at school, cheerfully left and got a job, were now being encouraged to stay at school – but still no job materialised. Youth unemployment figures remained disturbingly high throughout the 1990s. The radical change in the youth labour market that had been gathering momentum since the mid 1980s had reached dramatic proportions, seen in the 'precipitous' decline, post 1995, in the number of full-time jobs available to young people (Spierings 2003).

Schools were initially slow to re-gear their offerings to accommodate broader needs than addressed by the former academic subject listings. In the senior years, the traditional curriculum had been directed towards one thing, tertiary entrance. Now there were students in the senior classes who had no thought of further study – they simply had nowhere else to go. This situation was further compounded by changes to the various youth allowance requirements. Rather than leave school and go 'on the dole', by 1990 students were required to be in some form of study or training to qualify for a youth allowance. Not surprisingly then, the numbers in senior classes were swollen with young people whose presence was involuntary. Teachers were reluctant to give up their earlier ways of teaching – after all senior classes had traditionally been the jewel in the teaching crown. In this new environment, the senior years in some schools became more like survival tests for teachers, whose tasks involved catering to those wanting tertiary entry at the same time as trying to engage the others – disaffected and failing students – in some form of education. And although more boys leave school before completing the senior years, it is often those boys who stay on without any motivation for further study who form some of the groups of disaffected and failing students. These students actively resist schools' and teachers' efforts to get them to study, and disrupt opportunities for other students.

It is cause for concern that boys' retention rates are lower than those of girls. At the same time it must be recalled that the benefits of staying at school do not play out equally for males and females. For girls, leaving school early has been shown to be a much more significant disadvantage in terms of gaining employment than it is for boys. Summarising the findings of a major national study, Collins notes that in terms of labour force participation at age 24:

> Females who completed Year 12 did not have as good a chance of full-time work as males who left school early, let alone males who completed Year 12 ... completing Year 12 in and of itself is much more important to females than to males. (Collins 2000, p. 52)

Of course, this is not to say that it doesn't matter that some boys are leaving school early. Rather these findings demonstrate the complexity of the issues around education and gender and show particularly that gender impacts on the traditional connection between education levels and the capacity to find work.

The significant changes in university access, the senior school curriculum, the restructuring of the labour force and other consequences of globalisation continue to impact on the ways in which schooling works and the ways in which it is viewed. Young people's self-understandings, their identities which include their sense of being male or female, along with their conceptions of masculinity and femininity, are also changing in the light of different social conditions and cultural representations. The wave of concern about boys in school must be seen against this background if it is to be understood. Unfortunately, fanned by media hype about boys missing out, this concern has, at times, been presented as a 'battle of the sexes', predicated on notions of innate difference and pleading a 'special case' for boys often presented in terms of a fair go – girls have had it good and so now it's the turn of the boys.

Boys' education: the manufacturing of a 'crisis'?

As noted above, there are particular features of recent social changes and reconfigured schooling structures that have had consequences for the participation and achievement profiles of the senior school years. Several commentators have chosen to interpret these outcomes in terms of a systematic bias against males. These people have generated significant amounts of publicity in Australia and have connected with similar factions overseas, whose opinions are frequently quoted in the literature. Investigation of the boys' education platform demonstrates the following points:

1   **Not the same.** The constantly reiterated theme is that boys are 'different' – innately and fundamentally different in terms of their needs, their 'learning styles', their psychosocial development and their capacities. As noted in the previous chapter, the cognitive difference argument is difficult to sustain and is contradicted by a wealth of scientific evidence. One of the most serious problems with the difference thesis as a whole is that it presents all boys as the same – an intuitively unreasonable proposition and one that is not sustained by research evidence. The differences *among* boys are far greater than the differences *between* boys and girls on a vast range of measures.

2   **Not consistently based in high-quality research.** Much of the activity around boys' education currently stems from claims about essential qualities of boys, in contrast to the earlier push for girls' education, which was grounded in detailed research and analyses of how schools and classrooms typically work. On the topic of boys and schooling, the same names recur regularly in opinion pieces, publicity and keynote addresses. These spokespersons tend not to come from the same depth of evidence-based research that

accompanied the girls and education movement. While there is some excellent scholarship which addresses the area of boys and education, there are also a good many self-publicists whose presentations are often crafted from a potent mix of claims based on opinions, personal anecdote and mythologised experience, rather than carefully constructed research studies.

3 **Not a new story.** As noted above, the lack of school success of significant numbers of young Australian males is not a new development, but rather has been a consistent feature of the history of education in this country. School completion has become more important in the present time, but it is not equally important for males and females in assisting young people to find work.

4 **Not new teaching.** Seldom, if at all, do lists of strategies designed to promote boys' education differ in any substantive way from standard renditions of good teaching available in most pre-service and in-service teacher education courses and currently practised by good teachers in schools. Boys are to be encouraged to be articulate, empathetic, to express feelings and to operate in an environment free from harassment, as well as to be responsible and engaged members of the school community. Surely these qualities are to be seen as desirable for all students!

Notwithstanding the above qualifications, concern about boys' education has generated several government inquiries at both state and federal level and a large-scale DEST (Department of Education, Science and Training) commissioned study.[2] While at one level this activity and its associated publicity can be seen to contribute to the idea of boys as an area of special need in current Australian educational provision, there are some key insights that emerge. One is the government's evident concern to commit resources to provide for equity in education, a position which has led to the federal initiative to identify and award funds to 'lighthouse schools' which can demonstrate excellence in boys' education. Interestingly, of the 230 schools that were successful in winning grants, fewer than ten are single-sex schools – in this case of course, boys schools.

Another insight to emerge from the DEST study concerns the degree of theoretical overlap between some recent investigations of boys in schools and the earlier studies of girls' school experience (Lingard & Douglas 1999). Rather than view schools as over-feminised and women teachers as a central part of the problem for boys, this work takes the view that all the actors involved – teachers, students, school community – are culturally complicit in the production of certain sorts of masculinities and femininities. Analyses of this kind provide a much more fruitful starting point for interventions than the simplistic model of schooling acting in particular ways – or failing to act – on young people to produce pre-given outcomes.

Most of the publicity about boys and education adopts a less sophisticated approach. According to the boys in education lobby group, boys are the source of the major behaviour problems in schools – because their needs are not being met. In every Australian state statistics reveal that boys are being excluded or suspended far more frequently than girls. Boys, we are told, feel compelled to demonstrate 'being tough' at all costs (West 1998). Boys are too interested in sport, which then becomes detrimental to their studies; they are not doing their work in schools, are not doing it well enough, believe that 'real men don't read', nor do they participate in other academic pursuits (Stewart 1998). According to this lobby group, boys are 'naturally' aggressive and rebellious, slower to become literate, and more susceptible to self-deprecating behaviours that affect their health and educational development. Boys are 'falling behind girls academically in almost every subject' and 'leave school at a higher rate than girls' (IES Conferences 1998). Boys in education apologists often alert attention to the high suicide rate among young males and appear to believe that this, too, is a direct consequence of their schooling. The general message is that boys' education is in crisis. These issues have been vigorously taken up by the popular press, most especially in the reporting of end of school examinations.

End-of-school examinations and gender differences in achievement

During the past decade, when the annual end of school achievements are published, there has been an increasing reportage of girls 'outperforming' boys, of girls 'dominating' or 'outgunning' in the end of school results. Of course at one level it is interesting to note that for the many years when the reverse was the case there were no stories of boys 'dominating' or 'outperforming' – one can but assume that indeed their pre-eminence in academic achievement was interpreted as right and proper. Certainly terms such as 'dominating' or 'outgunning' appear to refer not simply to the fact that more girls pass the examinations, but that more girls are getting high scores in subjects that were previously boys' strongholds. Because of the ways in which subject selection impacts on straight comparisons it is difficult, if not impossible, to judge definitively what is happening 'behind the scenes'. Issues of where one draws the line in terms of deciding what level constitutes the top band are involved, as well as variables relating to student self-selection in terms of enrolment in particular subjects (this last with notable gender differences). A recent investigation of subject choice in senior school enrolments found clear trends relating to student gender and socioeconomic background. The report concludes:

> Gender was found to be one of the student characteristics accounting for the greatest proportion of variation in student enrolments. As found in previous subject choice reports, males predominate in the areas of Mathematics, particularly in higher level mathematics, physical sciences, technical studies, computer studies and physical education. Females predominate in the areas of English, humanities and social sciences, biological sciences, the arts, languages other than English, home sciences and health studies.
>
> Enrolments in Mathematics, and more particularly in the physical sciences, were found to be influenced by socioeconomic background as measured both by parents' occupations and by parents' educational levels. Enrolments were consistently higher in these subject areas for students from the higher socioeconomic background. Enrolments for the Technology Key Learning Area were consistently higher for those students from a lower socioeconomic background. (Fullarton & Ainley 2000)

While these general features have long been recognised, there are interesting crossover effects too. For instance, the maths–science subject areas continue to be more typical of male enrolment patterns than female and yet the girls who do take these subjects tend to do very well, probably because they are a more selected group. In popular media discussions of averages these important features disappear in the rush to grab a headline. While it appears to be true that more girls than boys pass their final examinations, some of the other claims are more dubious. Some examples:

- In 1998 in Queensland a greater proportion of girls than boys were in the top performance band in thirty-six out of forty-five subjects.
- In South Australia boys were underrepresented in the top performance band in twenty-seven out of thirty-four subjects in 1998. (Horne 2000)

In both these cases it is important to know just how the 'top band' was calculated. For instance, is it the top 5 per cent, 10 per cent; and is the gender effect constant at each percentile? Other examples:

- In Victoria the mean scores for girls were better than the mean scores for boys in thirty-five out of forty-one subjects.
- In New South Wales in 1998 the average score for boys was higher than the average score for girls in only three subjects: 2 and 3 unit computing studies and in mathematics in practice. (Horne 2000)

These statements do not necessarily indicate new and troubling information about gender equity. As noted earlier in the discussion of gender differences in intellectual functioning, averaging scores masks the within group variation as well as the different numbers of male and female students involved. For example, in the case of the examination results in physics in one state in 1994 the following trends were observed:

Of the 3627 students who participated, those with an A grade were 225 females (6.5 per cent of the total subject enrolment) and 430 males (11.9 per cent of the total enrolment), a result which might look as though the males' results were better, given that more of them scored in the top grade band.

However, of the 1155 females who entered, 19.5 per cent received an A (225 students) whereas of the 2472 males who entered 17.4 per cent received an A (430 students), which could suggest that females performed better.

Females made up just 31.8 per cent of the physics enrolments that year and were thus likely to be a more selected group than the males and so their 'better' scores could well be appropriate – not necessarily indicative of bias at all. (Gill 1995)

As can be seen from the above example, considerable care needs to be taken before claims of bias or unfair procedure are levelled on the basis of one take on the statistical profile of results. However, this sort of detail is not normally available through the popular press, which is all too often content to stick with stories of gender wars and unfair treatments. Unfortunately, these approaches have been recycled by the boys in education lobby, leading to the current sense of crisis regarding boys' education.

There are many things that could be said about the ways in which examination boards deal with school results in order to achieve tertiary ranking. In every state some elements of moderation or scaling are employed. One response to charges of gender bias could be to employ statistical techniques to 'wash out' elements that show one gender group as ahead of or behind the other. At this stage, rather than mask areas of gender difference, it seems preferable to continue to monitor the results in terms of the gender profile of students who enrol and their levels of outcome in order to construct achievement measures least prone to bias. A more important comment relating to the purported higher achievement of girls in the Year 12 examinations is that their 'domination' of the end of school examinations does not appear to lead to labour market advantage (Collins 2000). Although girls' end of school results appear better than those of boys as a group, this success is not followed through in terms of earning power and professional status in the post-school world.

There are, however, some relevant features of school achievement indicators that need to be considered here.

The examination factor

The ways in which the final school examinations are structured have significant gender implications. For many years, in every state external examinations were developed by the state's public examination body. All students sat a series of tests in traditional examination conditions and each student paper was assigned a score that was developed into a Tertiary Entrance Rank (TER) – more recently UAI – University Admission Index – calculated on the basis of their performance in these examinations. There was considerable variation between the states in terms of the degree to which examination scores were scaled and graded to offset particular biases and subject groupings. Some states used an ability measure against which the scores were moderated. The point for this book is that the system of public examinations underwent considerable modification in all states during the closing decades of the twentieth century. The general direction of the changes was in terms of an increased reliance on forms of assessment such as portfolio and project work, which meant that the student's score on the final examination was not the single determining factor for the tertiary entrance rank. In fact, now in many subjects examinations do not feature at all in the final result. Typically in Australian schools (as in the United States and United Kingdom), boys have been seen to perform better on examinations whereas girls often produced their best work in projects and assignments, completed without the pressure of examination conditions. Of course this feature does not hold for all boys and all girls and there are huge variations within either group, however the change in examination style was one that could be argued to suit one group more than the other – whereas under the previous system the reverse was true.

In addition, the way in which school certificates were structured was also associated with gender effects. The number of subjects that were required to complete the end of school certificate constituted another variable that impacted differently on male and female students. Whereas girls' enrolments are typically spread across a wide variety of subjects, boys tend to congregate in a much narrower range, with the double maths, physics and chemistry still a strong male pattern of enrolment. Hence girls are more likely to score highly on the ranking when a broad range of subjects is required whereas boys are more likely to do better when the range is restricted (Peck & Trimmer 1994). Education authorities must make decisions about how to construct end of school certificates that do not lend themselves to creating scenarios wherein either gender is advantaged. And schooling experience should afford students opportunities to undertake a range of assessments so that they can develop strategies to counteract undue pressures and yet remain accountable for their learning.

Thus there are some elements of changes in the end of school assessment structures which could be seen to relate to questions of gender equity. However, these issues hardly amount to an explanation for the degree of paranoia in the popular press about girls being unfairly advantaged in current educational arrangements. The discussion now turns to some of the more general concerns with boys' education.

Does 'boys' mean all boys, some boys, a few boys – which boys?

Most commentators agree that the situation with respect to boys and schooling should not be presented in terms of a homogenous gender category, but should rather be put in terms of which boys? (Teese et al. 1995; Gilbert & Gilbert 1998; Horne 2000). Despite these cautions, the lobby group continues to speak and write of boys as though there is a single category 'boys', with the implication that they are all the same – a necessary part of the 'fundamentally different' argument that is continually presented. It is true that some boys are not successful in school, some leave early, some are in trouble. And yet some others continue to do very well at school – as indeed some have always done. These are, in general, white middle-class boys who attend middle-class city-based schools where there is an academic curriculum and where they have the support of parents, teachers and the wider community (Teese et al. 1995). Boys continue to feature among the success stories of schooling, even if their successes, as compared with those of girls, are not as overwhelming a story as once was the case. A cursory inspection of the merit lists of high achievement routinely published in each state after the end of school examinations immediately reveals many boys among the top performers. While boys' high achievement is often connected to the maths–science subject groupings, it is not limited to this area. Nor is it apparently connected to attendance at a single-sex school.

The 'problem' of boys and education often centres on boys from less wealthy backgrounds for whom the promise of schooling appears very remote. The rate of school completion for these boys fell by over 13 percentage points from the early to mid 1990s (Lamb 1996). This trend appears to have continued, despite the fact that the nexus between school completion and having full-time work has been shown to be much tighter for boys than for girls (Collins 2000; McMillan & Marks 2003). For many boys from low socioeconomic backgrounds, schooling frequently means the requirement to participate in an experience for which they are unprepared in terms of attitudes, family background, resources – in other words they lack the cultural capital, a key factor in educational achievement. These boys correctly read the school situation as one in which they are destined to be unsuccessful. Their disruptive behaviour and refusal to conform to standard academic expectations can be seen as a product of their situation, not as a simple result of their being male.

Schools must develop new ways of engaging young people, male and female, in productive educational experiences, even if they do not intend to go into further education. Just because girls are tending to complete secondary school, it cannot be assumed that their educational experience serves them well – and it has been shown not to position them strongly in the search for full-time work. Similarly, because boys are leaving does not mean the education on offer is totally inappropriate. Rather it seems that the perceived rewards of schooling are not seen as attractive enough by considerable numbers of young men, especially those from poorer backgrounds.

This situation does present an intractable problem for the society.

Unless productive ways of involving young men in the social fabric are realised, we are looking at a society in which the old lines are no longer true and the new solutions are yet to be realised. The most recent Dusseldorp Skills Forum report on Australia's young people, *How Young People are Faring 2003*, revealed that around 15 per cent of teenagers are neither in full-time study nor in full-time work and that their chances of acquiring full-time work later on are slight (Spierings 2003). This finding is indicative of an increasing and systematic social stratification between those who have work and those who do not. It seems there is an urgent need for a reshaping of the education system. One approach could be to break the lockstep nexus between schooling and university entrance, and there are some indications that this has started to happen. The job of schooling then becomes one of introducing young people to the range of endeavours that have engaged previous generations as a good in its own right, not as a sorting mechanism for higher education, and not as a classifying treatment wherein some forms of learning are seen as better than others. This structure would leave the question of university admission to be solved by the universities themselves.

A different approach to the 'boys' question

It is important to note that not all commentators, researchers and academics who have taken up the issue of boys and their education are fuelled by the sense of boys having been unilaterally badly treated in terms of educational practices and outcomes. Some educational theorists have taken a position similar to that of the feminist theorists; that is, that many of the practices associated with 'normal' schooling carry messages about gender (for example, Gilbert & Gilbert 1998; Lingard & Douglas 1999). Not only do these practices construct femininity and masculinity, they also serve to monitor the forms of masculinity and femininity that are deemed acceptable. A 'macho' approach, often seen as the dominant or hegemonic form of Australian masculinity, is associated with being attention seeking, risk taking, oriented towards sporting achievement, displaying levels of aggression and so on. Dominant forms of femininity are constructed as oppositional to these attributes such that girls who embrace femininity are often seen as quiet, shy, timid, nurturing and so on. Schooling traditionally followed this strict gender division along a binary between 'rowdy' boys and 'quiet' girls. But there are other ways of being a boy and being a girl in school.

Indeed some research indicates that the policing of masculinity is often even more pronounced than that of femininity (Martino 1999). Hence it can be more acceptable for girls to engage in outrageous behaviour, or for a girl to be a sporting champion or a comedian, than for a boy to be overtly sensitive, to learn ballet, to shun football. What is needed then is for teachers and students to recognise these constructions as school-produced effects and to make confronting and challenging them part of the conscious effort of the school to produce young people free to fulfil their potential in any area of their choice.

Educational theory which has taken up the issue of boys and educa-tion from careful school-based studies has demonstrated the range of ways in which schooling typically predisposes some boys to act in ways that are counterproductive to academic achievement (Epstein 1998; Gilbert & Gilbert 1998). Masculinity is re-contextualised in schools such that call-ing out in class, showing off, denigrating intellectual achievement, behav-ing aggressively around girls, all becomes part of being a boy in school. What is needed then, according to these theorists, is the generation of pedagogic responses that engage with these behaviours and demonstrate their ineffectuality in the long term (Browne & Fletcher 1995). Some of this work details programs that are effective with boys which involve cre-ating space for boys to express their feelings, to admit to their fears and to recognise their weaknesses. Such approaches often resemble the rationale for education in literature and expressive arts – areas apparently not par-ticularly attractive to boys as seen in current subject enrolment profiles. The skills to be gained from these areas involve being articulate, commu-nicating clearly in speech and writing, being empathetic to others' responses, working collaboratively rather than in competition. All of these skills are strongly related to work in the new areas of service industries, hospitality and tourism and hence there could well be an employment enhancement for young men undertaking them. Could it be that the issues for boys in education are best met by designing an education more like that of girls? Rather than a separate issue – education and boys – could it be that what is needed for all our young people is simply good educa-tion, and of course its corollary good teaching?

Boys, girls and education: same, different or same difference?

Many of the claims put forward to sustain the idea that boys as a group are currently disadvantaged by schooling tend to mirror almost exactly the claims that were put forward in the 1970s and 1980s in which girls were seen as 'missing out' in education. For instance, whereas feminists had labelled standard schools as male institutions, the boys' lobby now presents schooling as overly feminised and as such producing a generation of disaffected boys who lack 'role models' (usually meaning male teachers), whose needs are not being met and who consequently are missing out on opportunities available to other students. With deliberate irony Eva Cox (1995) has dubbed this situation an example of a 'competing victim syndrome' in which the boys' education lobby seeks to demonstrate that currently boys are the most disadvantaged group, much more disadvantaged than girls. In other words, there is competition in the disadvantaged stakes and the boys are the most deserving bidders. Such an approach is both counterproductive and dangerous insofar as it suggests the distribution of educational benefits is a zero sum game in which, if there are gains to be made, they have to be at the expense of other players.

However, there are also significant differences between the platform of the boys' education lobby and that of the earlier girls and education movement. For instance, the claims about the girls being 'invisible' in standard schooling practice were supported by a range of research studies into the quality of their school experience. These studies had involved analyses of classroom talk (Spender 1980; Spender 1982), teaching treatments (Stanworth 1982), teacher recollection (Clarricoates 1980), student interviews (Milligan et al. 1992; Collins et al. 1996) and so on. The claims about boys missing out tend not to be drawn from an established research base, but rather are compilations of selected opinion, overwritten appeals to 'commonsense' and a good deal of emotive rhetoric. For example:

> Looking at the evidence which confronts us of so many young men suiciding, being suspended from school, in trouble on the streets and struggling to achieve at school, any sensible person would have to conclude that young males are in considerable difficulties. (West 2000, p. 2)

Moreover, the claims about the crisis in boys' education rarely reduce to boys being invisible. Rather more often, such accounts underscore boys' heightened visibility as a consequence of their disruptive behaviour, high levels of aggression and hostility, disengagement from school, truancy, being reported for misdemeanours, all of which is explained in terms of their needs not being recognised and catered for. Whereas some early and telling research had shown that teachers often did not know the names of the girls in their classes (Stanworth 1982), this was rarely true for boys. The point was made most succinctly by Yates, who roundly rejected the notion that it's now the boys' turn for special treatment in education:

> When teachers tell me that they can't get to sleep at night because they are worried about how to manage disruptive girls in their classes, how to develop curriculum that will keep their interest, how to survive in an environment constantly coloured by female hostility and aggression, then I will be ready to agree that girls are taking up more than their fair share of teacher concern. (Yates 1996)

There is a real need for educators to develop schooling processes that engage boys in learning more effectively than is currently the case. Rather than sorting out the brightest and best, contemporary schooling is rightly understood to be committed to the task of ensuring each student reach their maximum potential ('Adelaide Declaration' 1999, quoted in the Preface). There is no doubt that more needs to be done in the case of young people from disadvantaged backgrounds. Boys from poor backgrounds are particularly vulnerable because of the changes in the labour force, school class composition and examination treatments noted earlier. However, the case for boys as essentially different and needy does not appear to have been made convincingly – it tends to be a reiterated claim rather than the result of logical exposition.

Summarising the issues

The long-standing relation between schooling and work has undergone considerable modification in recent decades. Changes in the labour force, particularly the demise of extensive demands for manual labour, along with the decline in availability of full-time work, have meant that the ready option of leaving school early to find long-term employment is no longer available. Because of gender divisions in the Australian labour force, this change has appeared to impact more harshly on young men than on young women. However, female superiority in terms of school completion and success in final examinations is not reflected in post-school opportunities. Recent comprehensive analyses of school to work transition consistently show males, even those males who leave school early, are better positioned in terms of finding full-time work than are females (Collins 2000; McMillan & Marks 2003). Media-led campaigns which blame schools for failing boys have tended to simplify the problem as one of masculinity rather than seeing it as the logical consequence of broad societal change. This orientation – that is, towards the special needs of boys – has also been taken up by vocal members of the boys in education lobby.

There are of course some similarities with the situation that faced girls and women in education some twenty years earlier, in that schools were then faced with changing social arrangements and needed to ensure that they were preparing girls to enter the workforce in significant numbers. At the time the call was for more education for girls, higher retention, access to traditionally male subject areas and higher achievements. The set of issues around girls' education had gone largely unrecognised in the history of education in this country until some committed educators made public their concerns.

The proponents of the crisis in boys' education have a different agenda. For one thing, boys have never been shown to be rendered 'invisible' in standard teaching arrangements. The call now is for different educational treatments for boys who have not been denied access to prestigious subjects on the basis of gender, who have not been objectified and harassed routinely in their school experience, who have not been denied opportunities to complete school on the basis of gender. In other words, the campaign for special treatments and attention to boys' education derives from a different platform, one that is less informed by research than was the girls' education movement. Most crucially, whereas the pressure to improve girls' educational experience derived precisely from typical school arrangements and processes, the concern for boys' education as expressed by the boys' education lobby does not have the same relation to schooling situations.

Of course it is of concern to parents, educators and the wider public that some boys are disaffected at school, are failing, have need of remedial help at all levels, are seen as problems (particularly in secondary school) and are more prone to mental illness and suicide than girls at all levels. However, these are separate issues from the ones that drove educational improvements for girls and measures to counteract these problems must not be seen as 'taking back' the gains made for girls – although they are frequently presented in this manner.

It is of great significance that the problem facing boys has been identified as that of 'poor boys' – insofar as the boys who share the problems noted above tend to come from lower-middle and working-class backgrounds. These boys, who once had the ready option of leaving school to get a job, now languish in a system whose class-based design leaves them disaffected. Which brings us to the question: Would these boys do better in separate schools? Certainly the old prestigious boys schools which still operate along single-sex lines have not been vocal within the boys in education lobby. While a few voices within these schools have picked up on the idea of boys' education for boys, most are silent as they continue to present their client community with details of their considerable achievements in terms of examination results and university entrance, sporting prowess and illustrious 'old boy networks'. Could it be that the publicity around boys masks the class dimension in Australian education because it is more acceptable to talk about the intransigence of gender as a category and to smile and say 'boys will be boys' than to suggest that our education system is not working for significant numbers of our young people from underprivileged backgrounds, many of whom – but not all – are boys?

Educational theory has long identified the ways in which standard schooling practice becomes interrelated with the society it serves. Divisions in the wider society become reflected and refracted in the schools. A century ago it is clear that the qualitative differences in schooling for males and females reflected almost precisely the different life worlds of adult men and women of the time. This position constitutes another way of saying that education systems reflect the societies within which they are embedded, a point made early in this book. At the beginning of the twenty-first century it may be that the social distinction between rich and poor constitutes a clearer division in the wider Australian society than that between male and female. At this stage it is beyond the ambit of this book to suggest which is the wider gap or the greater divide. However, it is important to avoid the trap of focusing on gender, as the boys in education lobby has done, when in fact the evidence indicates that social class or, as perhaps seems most likely, some interrelation of the two, offers the most compelling explanation of the 'problem' of boys in school.

4

SINGLE-SEX SOLUTIONS?

Overview

This chapter provides an overview of the research relating to the benefits of single-sex schooling and reflects the early emphasis on girls' needs in this literature. Noting that all such work must be seen in terms of its particular context, this chapter identifies the key features relating to the positive effects that have been associated with single-sex schooling and comments on the degree to which school gender context is implicated in their achievement.

In the context of Australian schooling, girls schools in colonial times have not been represented as academies of learning so much as places for the training of ladies to fulfil their destiny as wives and mothers. Such a view was presented in early Australian classics such as *The Getting of Wisdom* and *Picnic at Hanging Rock*, both of which have been more recently celebrated in film. In these accounts Australian girls schools were seen to be discreet institutions wherein young ladies learnt socially appropriate decorum. As many of their names suggested, they were Ladies Colleges rather than girls schools. Their clientele was restricted, not simply by sex but perhaps more powerfully by the narrow social elite they served. The renewed attention to the idea of single-sex schooling for girls that came in the last quarter of the twentieth century was cast in a different mould, although strangely enough, in discussions and papers there is frequently talk of a 'return' to single-sex schooling.

The federal government line

When the idea of single-sex schooling was raised as a means of enhancing girls' education, the official position of the Commonwealth Schools

Commission on this topic reflected a good deal of ambiguity. Notwithstanding this, the official government line was to change significantly over the past two and a half decades. In 1975 in *Girls, School and Society* the position was put that single-sex schooling was 'the most fundamental expression of differing sex expectations ... ' (Commonwealth Schools Commission 1975, p. 63), a position which shows the writers' rejection of this form of schooling. However, later in the same document the commissioners wrote 'the issue [of single-sex schools versus coeducation] is still a live one requiring research' (Commonwealth Schools Commission 1975, p. 151). Nearly a decade later, in the 1984 report *Girls and Tomorrow: The Challenge for Schools* the position was even more ambivalent. Here the commissioners wrote:

> Single-sex schools are free from some forms of sexual harassment and are not subject to the territorial defence behaviours of boys ... In very powerful ways single-sex schools can still enforce messages about femininity and sex stereotypes through peer group and teacher pressure on girls who do not conform. At another level the lower fees set for girls schools as opposed to boys schools are an indication of the lower value set on girls' education.
>
> The single-sex versus coeducation debate will continue ... At present the most constructive and helpful approach appears to be for coeducational and single-sex schools to learn from each other and for each to implement, wherever possible, features of the other's environment which assist in the elimination of sexism from education. (Commonwealth Schools Commission 1984, p. 35)

It is clear from the terms of the above entry that the single-sex schools being discussed were in fact girls schools, a position so taken for granted that it was not felt necessary to spell it out. There appears to be more acceptance of the idea of single-sex schooling in this report than was evidenced in the earlier one. No doubt the publicity from feminist educators such as Dale Spender had influenced thinking on the matter and persuaded people of the need for girls-only schooling if girls were to achieve high academic results. Then, in 1987, *The National Policy for the Education of Girls in Australian Schools* included the following:

> The question of sex segregation as an educational strategy needs to be addressed more sensibly and seriously. (Commonwealth Schools Commission 1987, p. 27)

This comment indicates a more favourable stance towards single-sex schools as well as a degree of impatience with educational research in terms of its ineffectiveness in providing an answer to the question: Are girls better off in single-sex schools? By this stage there was a good deal of popular support from teachers and parents for the idea that single-sex education was a good approach for girls and this was reflected in the policy-makers' position. Meanwhile, other voices were suggesting that the 'single-sex solution' was a limited strategy in that it played to middle-class interests and was unlikely to affect the culture of the majority of students and teachers in coeducational schools (Kenway & Willis 1986). The trouble with the Commonwealth Schools Commissioners' position, as quoted above, was that the question does not lend itself to research which will show once and for all whether single-sex schooling is a solution for the girls and education issue – although there were efforts in this direction, which will be discussed shortly.

Through the 1980s the orientation in the gender and schooling literature was still very much single-sex schools from the point of view of girls' education – no mention here of single-sex schools for boys. And yet, as Phillips' work had shown, single-sex boys schools were producing young men with fairly unreconstructed ideas about men and women and life patterns, at the same time as similarly positioned girls school students expressed increasingly liberal views about their ambitions. While the boys at the elite boys schools envisaged a future with a beautiful wife who tended the children and the home, the girls from the girls schools planned university studies, travel and successful professional careers (Phillips 1980). Apparently the educational experience at these single-sex schools prepared young men and women for very different futures which, given the likelihood of these young people forming relationships within their shared social circle, would appear to be a recipe for domestic disaster.

The discussion now turns to the sorts of issues that were taken up by the research at this time. Themes concerning academic achievement, subject enrolment, personal development and career aspirations were all common. It is noteworthy that while there was a great deal of interest in the question of single-sex schooling for girls in Australia in the 1980s and early 1990s, research in the area appears to have diminished through the 1990s, except in particular areas such as maths–science education in which there continues to be a constant stream of studies.

A secondary school concern?

One immediately evident feature in discussions of single-sex schooling as compared with coeducation is that there is much more attention to the topic in terms of secondary school experience than elementary school. This limitation is curious since it has been shown that children in the primary school years do readily pick up understandings of gender appropriate behaviour and the need to conform to gender bounded norms. However, in primary school, the question of school gender context rarely arises. The vast majority of young Australians attend coeducational schools for their primary schooling. And they learn the ways of school, and of being male or female at school, in that environment. There is still anecdotal evidence of the gender wars that were once played out in many primary schools with chants such as:

Girls are weak, chuck 'em in the creek;
Boys are strong, like King Kong.

Although a familiar feature of previous times, such ritualised cultural gender segregation appears to have diminished significantly. In primary schools some girls still speak of the dangers of 'boy germs' if made to interact with an opposite sex peer and some teachers still use control mechanisms such as having their classes line up in opposite sex pairs or having boys and girls sitting together to make the class 'more manageable'. Overall, however, the impression is that there is less gender segregation at both the official and unofficial level in primary schooling than once was the case. There is, however, continuing evidence of school as a gendered experience.

An excerpt from some of my research is relevant here:

In a large study of primary school children's gender distinction in school behaviour, I was introduced to senior classes in a middle-class primary school as someone who was 'writing a book about school'. I then asked for the children's assistance with thinking up appropriate names for the characters in my story. The first question related to a student who was always in trouble, homework not done, answers not given, talking in class and so on – definitely not a good student. What shall I call this person? Of the 120 eleven- and twelve-year-olds involved in the study 98 per cent gave a boy's name for this student, confirming the popular impression that boys are more likely to be the naughty ones, the rule breakers, the poor students. (The three other names were comic characters of indeterminate gender – no-one gave a girls' name.) Even more comprehensively, when the children talked in small group interviews about the surprising fact that almost everybody had suggested a boy's name they said:

Jenny: I don't know why I put that ... I just did ...

Anna: You have to put something in and you choose the normal way it happens.

Lia: I didn't even think of putting a girl ... (Gill 1992a)

These responses suggest that this feature of typical boy behaviour – being in trouble – was one of those taken for granted aspects of school life, so common as not to be consciously registered. (Note that the implication is not that all boys are always in trouble, just that those who are in trouble are more usually boys.) Both boys and girls were equally likely to nominate a boy's name for the problem student. When asked to suggest a name for the good student in the story there was an interesting crossover effect with the boys once again proffering a boy's name while the girls almost all gave a girl's name. Would the responses have been similarly gender specific in a single-sex school? At this stage the question can't be answered.

While recent years have seen increasing numbers of non-government schools being established and there has been a good deal of concern raised about the 'drift' away from government schools, it remains the case that most Australian students (more than 97 per cent) begin their school days in coeducational schools. A relatively small proportion of them move to single-sex schools for their secondary education, the majority stay in coeducation, in one or other of the school systems for all their schooling. The non-government sector attracts larger numbers of students at the secondary level than the primary level. The following table shows the increase in numbers of non-government school students between 1985 and 1995, the differences between primary and secondary level enrolment in single-sex schools in the non-government sector and also the decline in numbers of single-sex schools within this sector.

By 1995 less than a quarter (24.2 per cent) of students in non-government schools attended single-sex schools. By 2002 the non-government schools accounted for just 32 per cent of the total school population, therefore under 8 per cent of the total school population attended single-sex schools. As revealed in the above table, single-sex schooling accounted for a significantly higher proportion of students at secondary level than at primary level, which forms another feature of the enrolment profiles of such schools. The current picture of single-sex schooling in Australia is comprised of a small number of primary single-sex students (2.2 per cent of the whole school population) together with a small proportion of students from the coeducational majority of primary schools across all school sectors moving to a single-sex school for their secondary education.

Table 4
Students attending non-government schools

School type	1985 Primary %	1985 Secondary %	1985 Total %	1995 Primary %	1995 Secondary %	1995 Total %
Single-sex	8.6	54.8	30.7	6.9	43.3	24.2
Male	6.1	27.3	16.2	3.6	20.7	11.7
Female	2.5	27.5	14.5	3.3	22.6	12.5
Coeducational	91.4	45.2	69.3	93.1	56.7	75.8
Total	100.0	100.0	100.0	100.0	100.0	100.0
Total students '000	403.1	367.9	770.9	471.6	428.3	899.9

Source: Australian Bureau of Statistics (ABS) (1997), *Australian Social Trends*, p. 72.

The move from one school experience to another may have different effects on different students. Girls moving to a girls school from a coeducational primary school in my study reported 'missing the boys' as a salient feature of their experience at the new school, although two years later they appeared to have completely acclimatised to an all-female student environment. In my thesis I argued that these girls appeared to have taken on the role of passive watchers in their coeducational primary school and they spoke fondly of the fun they had enjoyed 'watching the boys' who used to 'get up to such naughty things'. The move to a single-sex school had entailed significant change in their understanding of the ways of school, which had previously been strongly marked by gender. No research has been carried out to date on the effects on boys of moving from a coeducational experience to an all-boys school.

Most studies of the effect of school gender context have looked at subject enrolment and academic achievement in the senior years of school as providing indicators of schooling success. Such indicators are much more available in terms of secondary schooling than of primary school and hence the high school years have been the focus of much of this research. At the same time, it is important to register that this is a limitation of much of the research evidence, in that it discounts primary school experience. In addition, studies of subject enrolment and achievement outcomes could be seen to reduce schooling effects to a very narrow band of categories. A minor theme in research on school gender context, and one that is not so limited, concerns research into student self-esteem, general well-being and social maturity. While there are interesting studies in these areas, they have not been reported to the same extent as studies of student achievement levels and enrolment patterns.

The current provision

The current provision of single-sex secondary education within Australian schooling is mostly limited to the non-government sector, except in the state of New South Wales where, at the secondary level, there are still 24 girls schools, 22 boys schools in addition to 346 coeducational schools. There are no single-sex government schools in Queensland or Western Australia, however Tasmania has one girls secondary school, South Australia has two and Victoria currently has eight girls high schools. In general, public primary schools are coeducational, as are the vast majority of the smaller non-government schools that cater to primary level enrolments. A pattern of increasing adoption of coeducation in the non-government sector has evolved over the past two decades, which have also seen the demise of government supported single-sex schools (once the preserve of the technical high schools) in the general move towards comprehensivisation – a trend in which once again Australian education followed the British system. The numbers of such schools within each state are presented in table 5.

From these figures it is clear that there are more girls schools than boys schools across states and school sectors, with the Catholic sector continuing to provide more single-sex schools than either the government or the non-government systems. This difference in favour of girls schools probably reflects the popular impression that girls achieve more highly in girls-only schools. The numbers of such schools in each state vary beyond what could be expected to arise from differences between state populations. Even discounting the larger population of New South Wales, there are notably more single-sex schools in this state, possibly inspired by the larger government provision of such schools. However, the proportions of students in single-sex schools has been declining steadily as a result of the trend to coeducation in some of the former single-sex established schools and the development of new non-government schools.

Table 5
Single-sex secondary schools in Australia, 2002

	Government		Non-government		Catholic		Totals
	Boys	Girls	Boys	Girls	Boys	Girls	
ACT	–	–	1	1	2	2	6
NSW	22	24	13	22	30	31	142
Qld	–	–	10	16	11	23	60
SA	–	2	2	5	6	9	24
Tas.	1	1	1	2	1	2	8
Vic.	1	8	12	21	13	23	78
WA	–	–	7	5	2	5	19
Totals	24	35	46	72	65	95	337

Source: Compiled from Department of Education, Science and Training (DEST) statistics, 2002.

Note: There are no single-sex schools in the Northern Territory.

Certainly the majority of the newly established non-government schools are coeducational, significant numbers of which have been showing a rapid expansion. While many of the traditionally established schools continue to be single-sex, more former boys schools have adopted coeducation than has been the case with former girls schools. It would appear that the prospect of a boy going to what was formerly a girls school is a more difficult proposition than that of a girl going to a former boys school. It could also be that the traditional boys schools are seen as having greater drawing power within the prospective client community than the girls schools, although many of the former boys schools have trouble reaching the 50/50 mark in terms of equal numbers of boys and girls; in many cases the proportion of girls is less than 50 per cent. The reasons behind these moves to coeducation are often a complex mixture of financial management, market response and educational principles. On the latter question, it seems that more parents and educators are willing to accept the idea that having girls in the classroom and the school will be good for the boys than to see boys in the class as good for girls, a perception that recalls the comment of the headmaster of one of the long-established British boys schools:

> Marlborough will always be a boys' school ... and it will be a better boys' school for having a few girls in it.

This still begs the question: What is the best schooling for girls?

Meanwhile, the non-government girls schools maintain the benefits of girls-only schooling and construct their advertising accordingly. The boys schools are less inclined to market themselves on the basis of boys needing an all-boys environment to do well in school. More frequently, they trade on their established name, their long list of former students who have become public figures and their demonstrable success in terms of university entrance. For example, one such school proudly lists on its website:

> From the bluestone classrooms of [XXX] Grammar have come three Prime Ministers, Antarctic explorers, over one hundred Anglican clergy, the first Australian artist to be admitted to the Royal Academy, distinguished servicemen, academics, business-men, industrialists, members of professions, musicians, actors, politicians, farmers, and many other Australians who have all made their contribution to this country's growth.

The gender composition of the school remains unstated in this account-ing and yet it is implicitly understood that this is a boys school, dedi-cated to preparing young men to take up impressive public careers.

From the outset, Australian educational research into the question of single-sex schooling versus coeducation was concerned with girls' schooling and the girls schools were quick to take up their newfound celebrity by making their status as single-sex institutions an explicit part of their self-promotion. The media are happy to play along with the trend. 'Girls better without boys' (the *Adelaide Advertiser* 15/07/03, p. 11), 'Single-sex schools on comeback' (the *Age* 22/10/02, p. 3) are just some of the recent headlines in the popular press on this issue.

Single-sex schools – a girls' movement?

The girls in education movement that began in the 1970s stimulated interest in the question of single-sex schooling as connected with girls' educational achievements. Just prior to this, a well publicised British study conducted over several years had come out in favour of coedu-cation as promoting 'optimal adjustment to life' (Dale 1969, 1971, 1974), but, given that it was a time of significant changes in gender pat-terns of work and life, it is perhaps not surprising that feminists were quick to take issue with the findings.[1] Re-analysis of Dale's data pur-ported to show that for girls, high academic achievement was connec-ted to attendance at an all-girls school (Harding 1981; Shaw 1981).

A flurry of studies in the United Kingdom followed, most of which confirmed the idea of single-sex schools being associated with high female achievement, with girls being more likely to enrol in the prestigious maths and science subjects (even though the girls schools were less well resourced than coeducational schools or boys schools), with girls occupying senior roles in student government, with girls prepared to take up non-traditional careers and so on (Cowell 1981; Harding 1981; Shaw 1981; Stanworth 1982; Delamont 1983; Deem 1984; Harvey 1984, 1985). This work was widely reported and gathered publicity in Australia, given the upsurge of interest in questions of girls' education.

The British government, through the Department of Education and Science (DES), commissioned two large-scale studies in the early 1980s to investigate the claims about the benefits of single-sex schooling for girls (Bone 1983; Steedman 1983). The results of both studies supported the conclusion that the high female achievement was not due to the school being single-sex or coeducational but rather was mainly accountable in terms of the style of school – whether it was a grammar school or a comprehensive or secondary modern – with high achievement being closely associated with the overtly academic grammar school. Other relevant variables associated with high achievement included the aspirations of the girls and their parents, their parents' level of education, their socioeconomic status and student ability, as measured prior to entering the school. What these studies showed was a complex interaction of factors associated with student outcomes, with academic achievement being clearly connected to measured ability and academic orientation of the school – for both girls and boys. While noting a tendency for more girls to study the maths and science subjects in single-sex schools than in coeducational schools, the researchers found that girls who did undertake these subjects in coeducational schools tended to perform more highly than the girls in single-sex schools. Taken together, the results of these studies supported the conclusion that the school gender context in or of itself was not significant in terms of producing high academic achievements for girls. Notwithstanding this conclusion, the proponents of single-sex schooling for girls have continued to affirm the position that female academic achievement derives from attendance at an all-girls school. Some claim that girls can only do well if they attend a girls school (see Spender quoted in the Introduction). Currently in Australia this perception has become part of the popular mythology of schooling, and as such forms the background for some of the following research.

Following the British work, a range of Australian studies investigated the question of school gender context in relation to female academic achievement. In the overwhelming number of cases the results were inconclusive. There were inherent design problems in this work insofar as it was impossible to test the same girls with the same teachers across differently organised schools in any one study. The Australian researchers were not able to assess students on the basis of ability before the girls attended school. And there were several features specific to Australian education systems that made the question even more complicated.

In this country the distinction between single-sex schools and coeducational ones sits on top of the distinction between government and non-government schooling. By the 1980s, most states had ceased to provide significant numbers of single-sex schools within the public school systems – the exceptions being New South Wales and Victoria, which continue to have some girls-only secondary schools, twenty-four and eight respectively. Hence, for those not living in suburban Sydney or Melbourne, going to a girls school nearly always meant going to a non-government or 'private' school, popularly understood as indicative of higher educational aspirations and achievement, parental choice and higher socioeconomic status. As noted in chapter 2, the connection between academic achievement and attendance at a non-government school had become one of the established features of Australian educational provision, largely because attendance at such schools also meant membership of the middle class, with its attendant privileges such as educational resources, emphasis on parental support for and encouragement of children's achievement, in addition to higher levels of parental education. A particular school being girls-only may not have been nearly as important as the fact that it was part of this established company, in addition to which, several of the girls schools had rigorous selection procedures which ensured that only the brightest and the best passed through their domain. Despite the lack of research confirming the benefits of single-sex schools for girls, the relation between single-sex schooling and girls gaining impressive academic results has been maintained in the popular mind, even if no direct causal connection has been established.

Claims and impressions

Talking with the girls in the government girls school which formed one context for my study of gender and schooling, the question of school choice arose. When asked why the particular girls school had been chosen the girls in my study gave a range of answers, including:

> Jeannie: Well mum really wanted me to come here. You see she wanted me to go to one of those posh schools but she couldn't afford it. But here you see it's almost like a private school ...

> Rosa: Yeah ... my parents think I will learn to be more ladylike at this school, not like some of those tough schools near us ... (Gill 1992a)

As can be seen in this example, it was not the single-sex quality of the school that was sought so much as the 'good school', part of the established academic and social elite whose schools had traditionally been single-sex.

As a result of the dual system of schooling in Australia, the fee-paying school has become, in the public mind, virtually synonymous with a 'good school'. For instance, anecdotal accounts confirm that what many parents desire most for their children is to give them the benefit of a 'good education' at one of the nation's prestigious fee-paying schools. This perception is attested to and augmented by establishments such as the Australian Scholarships Commission (ASC), which runs regular advertisements in the popular press to encourage parents to 'do the right thing' by their children, which is understood by this group to mean buying them an education. While many of these non-government schools may well be excellent schools and comprise teachers who are dedicated and inspiring, their success clearly also derives from the selection built into their client community. By charging fees they are distinguishing themselves from the government system and hence select for people who are able and prepared to pay large amounts of money for the education of their children.

While not wanting to suggest that this selection process is foolproof and operates in a blanket way – not all non-government school students achieve highly and there are of course considerable numbers of parents who value education, who are themselves well educated and who deliberately elect to send their children to government schools where they do very well – it does serve to reinforce the connection between fee-paying schools and high achievement. And the issue of single-sex schooling sits on top of this connection. The work of the non-government girls schools – and sometimes their explicit publicity – serves to cement the impression that attendance at a girls-only school is necessary for high academic achievement for girls.

And the research?

The question of the best way to school for girls and boys is evidently neither clear cut nor simple due to the myriad of interacting factors. If one were to look back to the mid twentieth century, say, it would appear that the single-sex schools had a fairly clear advantage in terms of producing high-achieving young men and women. Not only did many more of their graduates go on to university, the vast majority of men and women in significant public positions had been educated at such schools. The degree to which the schools' single-sex composition was central to the production of such strong academic achievement is, however, not proven. While it is clear that statistically there was a high correlation between attendance at a single-sex school and proceeding to university, it cannot be inferred that the school context alone produced these outcomes. In addition, that degree of correlation has substantially weakened in recent decades, along with increased retention rates in coeducational government schools and the increasing number of non-government coeducational schools.

Historically, many of the academically oriented schools were in the non-government sector, however there were also some single-sex government schools among the schools sending high achievers to university. The system of selective, single-sex, government schools was enjoying its heyday around the 1950s and 1960s. For instance, in terms of girls schools there was MacRobertson Girls in Melbourne, Fort St in Sydney, Adelaide Girls' high school and so on. These schools were equally, if not more, renowned for their high levels of student achievement when compared with the non-government girls schools. And they too were single-sex. The widespread adoption of comprehensivisation within the government sector schooling has meant the demise of most such selective entry schools, along with that of the technical schools. The question of the 'best way to school' has become much more complicated.

One of the first Australian studies that attempted to comprehensively investigate any causal connection between single-sex schooling and girls' academic achievement was carried out in 1985 by Peter Carpenter (Carpenter 1985). Despite a healthy sample size across two states and a battery of tests, any conclusions to be drawn from this work must be somewhat tentative. From the outset Carpenter stressed the need to be aware of the multiplicity of confounding variables, most fundamentally that the issue of single-sex schooling in most parts of Australia operates as a subset of another school-reflected social division, namely that of public versus private schooling. Within each school sector there was a range of variables other than being single-sex or mixed, and these different dimensions were seen to be also likely to impact on student achievement. Not surprisingly then, Carpenter's conclusions were somewhat mixed. For instance, he found that girls from single-sex schools were more likely to do science but that those from coeducational schools who do science are more likely to be highly successful. (At the time of the study, 1985, there was an even stronger connection between studying science at senior years and being part of the school's academic elite than is the case now.)

Carpenter was especially careful to interrelate socioeconomic factors with school and achievement outcomes, and much of this carefully written paper attests to an awareness of these interrelationships. Thus it seems that the gains from one or other type of school may be different depending on the socioeconomic level of student background – girls from poorer families might be advantaged in a single-sex school, whereas those from middle-class backgrounds may not be affected by school gender context in terms of their academic achievements. There are intriguing suggestions about school effects too, as in 'girls do well in Year 12 if they believe strongly in their academic ability, but the advantages of this mechanism are much greater in single-sex schools than in coeducation' (Carpenter 1985, p. 470). Such comments suggested the need for more qualitative studies of schooling processes in order to investigate the proposed connections.

In all, Carpenter's study made it abundantly clear that there were no clear or immediate gains for girls in terms of achievement from attendance at either single-sex or coeducational schools. Effects of school gender context were seen to be interrelated with other variables and not strongly implicative on their own.

Carpenter's conclusions of no clear effect of school gender context echoed those of Barboza (1983) who had investigated student attitude to mathematics across two high schools – one coeducational, the other single-sex – and concluded that single-sex environment alone is not a sufficient influence to counter girls' perceptions of mathematics as a male-dominated area of intellectual endeavour. Subsequent researchers have identified a good deal of difference within the categories single-sex and coeducation – more so than between them (Hunter 1987). In other words there is considerable variation within single-sex schools and within coeducational schools, so much so that to conduct testing as though gender context were the one significant difference would be to build on a flawed proposition.

A further large study, which looked at the relationship between school type and attitudes to careers and self-esteem, was carried out in a number of Victorian schools by Ditchburn & Martin (1986). Once again the study did not produce any clear overall recommendation or conclusions in terms of a causal relationship between one or other type of school and a particular outcome. It did, however, register concern at the lower self-esteem of the girls, regardless of school type, at their lower career aspirations and their under-representation in the maths–science classes, the latter two effects being more pronounced among the girls from coeducational schools than the single-sex ones. It is noteworthy that the single-sex schools involved in the Ditchburn & Martin study were in the Catholic school sector and did not include the high socioeconomic status elite girls schools. Their finding of girls' lower self-esteem is picked up in the later research into self-esteem and school gender context, an area that forms one of the themes of research on this subject.

More recent work which investigated career aspirations has indicated that the type of school females attend (coeducational government, coeducational non-government, single-sex non-government) does not influence students' career-related attitudes and expectations (Stent & Gillies 2000). The interesting finding from this study was that both males and females had shifted away from traditional career attitudes and that occupational stereotyping by both genders has been greatly reduced. Such a result indicates the dynamic changes in gender roles that have been a feature of the wider society in recent years.

The two large Australian studies described above reinforced the conclusions drawn from the large-scale British research that had shown that school gender context was not a significant variable in terms of affecting student outcomes. Subsequently, smaller studies conducted with individual schools were carried out to investigate particular lines such as student self-esteem, science enrolment, career aspirations and so on, the results of some of which are less indicative of 'no difference' when compared with the large-scale ones noted above.

A recent study from New Zealand stands against the general trend for research to show no effect of school gender context. Using an eighteen-year longitudinal study of a birth cohort of 657 New Zealand children, the researchers were able to show a clear positive effect of single-sex schooling on a number of educational outcomes (Woodward et al. 1999). This study is interesting for at least two reasons relevant to the current discussion. First, the benefits of single-sex education held true for boys as well as girls, and as such this a relatively unique result in terms of the writing about boys and education. Secondly, given that New Zealand has a broadly established tradition of government girls schools and boys schools, this result could indicate once again the importance of cultural context. If school climate in the single-sex schools were to be more academic than at the coeducational schools (as has been suggested by some researchers) the positive effect could be explained as a result not simply of school gender composition but of the interaction with an academic school climate. While the older tradition in New Zealand was to have single-sex high schools, such schools continue to hold to more academic culture than the more recent coeducational high schools (Harker & Nash 1997; Hill 2003). Hence the reported results could be read as indicating once again that the academic style of the school may be a more important variable than its gender composition.

It is noteworthy here that in an earlier larger study of over 5000 New Zealand junior high school students (Harker & Nash 1997), the researchers found some indication in the raw data of an advantage to girls in single-sex schools. However, when the data were controlled for ability levels, social and ethnic backgrounds and mix at the two types of schools, the initial differences disappeared. The authors concluded that 'the difference in average academic attainment of girls who attend single-sex schools as against coeducational schools is more apparent than real'. The phrase 'more apparent than real' appears to summarise the current situation regarding girls' academic performance and the degree to which it is directly produced by attendance at a single-sex school.

Subject choice and the maths–science strand

One line of research into the question of potential advantages of single-sex schools has concentrated on the area of subject choice, given the early findings that girls' choices appear more restricted and gender typed in coeducation. It was argued that the coeducational school tended to polarise subjects into girls' areas and boys' areas and thus both male and female students undertook gender typical subjects, which meant girls doing history and languages and boys doing science and mathematics. Certainly the early British research had shown that in single-sex schools more boys and girls chose subjects on non-traditional gender lines (Ormerod 1975). A range of Australian research carried out in the 1980s and 1990s tended to reinforce these findings, albeit with some interesting variations.

A 1998 study showed that Australian girls do tend to see mathematics as a male domain and have typically less positive attitudes to mathematics as a subject area than do boys (Norton & Rennie 1998). This study also found that school type, either single-sex or coeducation, had only a small effect on the girls' attitude to mathematics; the effect of their gender was much more pronounced. In other words, girls were inclined to see maths as male appropriate and not female appropriate, regardless of the sort of school they attended.

Young (1994) found that girls in single-sex schools were more likely to choose physics, but that the effect of home background was a much more important factor in student achievement than type of school.

Bornholt (1991) found that single-sex schooling appeared to reduce the influence of traditional gender stereotypes for both boys and girls, but that the interaction between student gender and subject domain produced different effects for males and females. These results confirmed the earlier study of Foon (1988) who had found that the type of school attended did have consequences in terms of adolescents' stated preferences and rated achievements. Foon's study had revealed that students attending coeducational schools had more traditional subject preferences and assessments of achievements in those subject areas than students attending single-sex schools.

However, Hunter's research (Hunter 1987) into the same area had shown that there was more variation within each of the school categories than between them – a finding which cautions against any quick generalisation about school gender context effects in terms of subject choice. Similarly, a West Australian study had found strong school effects in subject choice which in some cases counteracted the gender stereotyping (FitzPatrick & Brown 1983), an important finding in that it suggests that schools can consciously intervene to broaden student aspirations and related subject and career choices.

Overall there is evidence that girls' subject choices have tended to be less traditionally gender typed in single-sex schools but that all schools, both coeducational and single-sex, can consciously intervene in the area of subject choice to effect a less stereotypical profile.

Much of the research on single-sex schooling compared with coeducation has been centred on mathematics and science as subject areas in which typical gender divisions in terms of enrolment choices, attitudes and achievement levels are intertwined. Studies in this area are spread across investigations of different school types and those of differently organised classrooms. One of the clearest findings in favour of single-sex schooling for girls was produced by Yates & Firkin (1986) who found that single-sex schools had both higher levels of achievement and lower levels of failure in senior school mathematics examinations. While student gender was seen as strongly connected to participation in senior school mathematics, attendance at a single-sex school was even more strongly connected to outstanding success. An interesting feature of this study was that it showed roughly equal proportions of girls undertaking mathematics across the three socioeconomic levels into which the group was divided. As the authors note: 'The low participation of girls remains constant across socioeconomic status and school type (that is, government and non-government) suggesting that gender is a stronger determinant of participation than either of these factors' (Yates & Firkin 1986, p. 18).

Several other studies in the 1980s attested to the advantages for girls' achievement in terms of studying maths in single-sex schools or classes (Ballenden et al. 1984; Dunn et al. 1984; Friedlander 1985; McMillan et al. 1985; Rowe et al. 1986). During this time the campaign to encourage girls to study mathematics at senior levels was in full swing.

This line of inquiry – between school or classroom gender context and participation and achievement in mathematics and science – has continued through the past decade as one clear thread within this complex area of research. Because of the demonstrable gender difference in the uptake of maths–science subjects in senior school, it presents as an important area in which to attempt to detect school-based effects.

A series of studies has been carried out over the past decade that investigated gender context effects on girls' participation and achievement in science in Western Australia (Parker & Rennie 1997; Parker & Rennie 2002). The ambit of this project, SSEPP (Single-sex Education Pilot Project), has been to explore the climate generated within the single-sex classroom in terms of its enabling female participation and achievement. In these careful studies the researchers are not oriented towards making a definitive conclusion about one or other type of classroom as being preferable. Rather they report on the range of interacting variables which impact on student outcomes. While noting that teachers experience single-sex classrooms as more conducive to gender inclusive instructional strategies, they also readily noted that the beneficial effect of the classroom grouping depended in the first instance on the teachers' commitment to the SSEPP program, and also that of the parents, the students and the wider school community. Other research has reached similar conclusions (Leder & Forgasz 1997). For example, girls whose teachers and parents believed they would be better off in a single-sex classroom were more likely to benefit from that arrangement than were girls whose parents and teachers did not think it would make a difference. Such findings echo the phenomenon that has been labelled the 'self-fulfilling prophecy', in which the belief that a certain condition is connected to specific outcomes will tend to produce those outcomes. This element has continuously bedevilled research into the effects of school gender context.

In a study that looked particularly at student and teacher attitudes to mathematics classes in terms of gender contexts, Rennie & Parker (1997) demonstrated that both teachers and students viewed single-sex classes as providing a more supportive environment for girls, but less so for boys. This finding would appear to suggest that an intervention strategy, such as the setting up of single-sex classes within the coeducational school, may work best when it is directed against the grain of established attitudes. For instance, it could be that single-sex classes for boys in literature may be seen as producing a more supportive environment for boys in a subject that is not a strong area of male enrolment. Certainly some of the claims made by researchers investigating boys' education have lauded single-sex classes as strategies that are designed to appeal to boys in teaching English and humanities subjects, whereas others have argued that the gender context is not nearly as important as the quality of the teaching (Martino & Meyenn 2002). Other studies which have investigated the use of single-sex classes for particular subjects have shown a boost in student confidence and achievement, but these positive outcomes tend to have been short lived and would appear to reflect a novelty effect rather than a long-term benefit.

In terms of mathematics being seen as a male domain, several studies through the 1990s demonstrated that girls in single-sex schools were less inclined to stereotype mathematics than were girls in coeducational schools (Jones & Young 1995; Rennie & Parker 1997). Several studies into the effects of setting up single-sex classes 'for girls' in maths and science report some gains in the short term, but researchers are very cautious about imputing any long-term effects (Morrow 1991; Rowe et al. 1986; Rowe 1988). Other researchers have cautioned against an ideology of 'single-sex classes for girls in maths and science', suggesting that the very labelling of such study groupings carries the implication that girls are typically deficient in these areas and hence require special treatment and protection (Gill 1992b). As has been noted in previous chapters, the early work on girls' education had a tendency to portray girls in terms of a deficit model, as lacking in motivation, achievement orientation, capacity for abstract thought and so on. This perspective has been theoretically discredited in favour of viewing girls as picking up the idea of being a girl and not strong in certain subject areas as a result of school experience. There are traces of the earlier ideas – that girls' identities and capacities are weaker, deserving of protection – in some of the writing in favour of single-sex schools and classrooms.

A recent large-scale Australian study published in an international collection (Ainley & Daly 2002) provided the latest overview of girls' enrolment in physics and related achievement in terms of their attendance at single-sex or coeducational schools. Once again, the research failed to show a significant relationship between school type and academic outcomes, even in this subject, physics, which has maintained its traditional male-dominated enrolment patterns despite the decline in its overall enrolment. Physics, it seems, has become less popular with both male and female students in recent years and its uptake by girls in girls schools is no stronger than by girls in mixed schools.

Another line of research into the potential effects of school gender context has concerned the question of student self-esteem, already seen as associated with gender difference in favour of males.

Studies of school change and student self-esteem

One of the most telling examples of research into school gender context was the comprehensive study conducted by Marsh and a team from the University of Sydney into the merger of two formerly single-sex schools in an area just south of Sydney. Reports of this study (Marsh et al. 1986; 1988; Marsh 1989) demonstrate many positive effects of the merger. After an initial decline in measured levels of self-esteem, all students developed more positive attitudes to themselves and to their school. Student achievement, of both girls and boys, appeared to have been boosted by the merger, as did their general positive orientation to the new school and themselves as its students.

It was particularly noteworthy that the achievement levels of the girls increased in their new environment – *even though the teachers had expected the reverse to be the case.* This finding is most interesting in that it demonstrates the fact that gender is caught up in the dynamic social flux in which women's and men's roles and expectations around those roles are continuing to change and adapt to new social conditions. Whereas in the 1970s researchers had been disturbed to discover that teachers held higher expectations for boys than girls and assumed that the differential outcomes were produced at least in part by these teacher expectations, the young people in this study were shown not to conform to the gender role expectations of their teachers. The changing nature of gender roles further complicates research into the effects of school gender context and makes it even less likely that a definitive answer will arise.

A follow-up study of self-esteem at the school ten years later revealed that the improvement in self-esteem had been maintained for both boys and girls post merger (Smith 1996). In other words the merger was connected to positive schooling outcomes for all concerned.

Similarly, a series of studies of student self-esteem and school climate following the adoption of coeducation by two former non-government boys schools in South Australia showed an eventual increase in self-esteem levels (after an initial dip) and a more positive student perception of school climate (Yates 2001; Yates 2002). While there is a need to be aware of the potential of a Hawthorne effect[2] with school change – which would explain the positive results in terms of the boost in performance when people become conscious of being monitored – it seems a reliable body of evidence is being developed that supports the idea of a move to coeducation as a largely positive experience for all involved.

Post-school adjustment

Many of the proponents of coeducation claim that its 'naturalness' and congruence with normal living arrangements constitute important reasons for commending it as an educational strategy. The point is made in contrast to single-sex schools, which are described as outdated seminaries or hothouses of sexual repression. A further line of research that has attempted to evaluate the different outcomes from single-sex schools as compared with coeducation has been investigations of former students in terms of their post-school choices. Early findings in Britain, for example (Dale 1969, 1971, 1974), which had come down in favour of coeducation, were based, at least in part, on the proposition that coeducation laid the 'best preparation for life'. In Australia in 1986, Harris conducted a large-scale survey of young people's adjustment to university related to their school experience (Harris 1986). She found that those who had been educated at a coeducational school made the smoothest transition in terms of ease of interactions with the opposite sex, a finding that was in line with Dale's conclusions. In terms of academic outcomes, however, Harris found no significant difference between types of school attended.

Another study of university enrolments found that students from single-sex schools were more likely to enrol in the professional courses of law and medicine whereas those from coeducational schools were more strongly represented in fields of engineering and science (Baldwin 1990a). However, as the author notes, this result is most likely a reflection of the advantaged background of the single-sex, non-government school graduates rather than a dimension brought about by their schooling experience. In a second study of first-year university students, Baldwin (1990b) had found that many of the female engineering students, who were very much a minority gender group in their engineering class, accounted for their high achievement and their non-traditional career choice in terms of having attended a single-sex school. These young women claimed that their single-sex school experience had given them the confidence to pursue non-traditional school subjects and related careers. However, given that high achievement and non-traditional careers were very much in line with the claims made by such schools, it is difficult to accept their accounts uncritically. In keeping with studies showing female readiness to externalise responsibility for success, as shown in the work on locus of control (Dweck 1980), it may have been easier for these young women to explain themselves in terms of factors other than their own capacity, drive and determination. Most probably some combination of high ability and a supportive learning environment and family background would seem to offer the most accurate explanation.

Summarising the research findings

Taken together, the conclusions to be derived from these research studies do not support the claim that female academic achievement requires a single-sex school environment. While the concerns about girls' potential to choose gender-typed subjects, their avoidance of the maths and physical sciences, and their tendency to lower self-esteem when compared with boys are all cause for concern, there are some indications that girls from single-sex schools are less vulnerable on these dimensions. However, it has not been shown that the gender context of the school is sufficient in or of itself to outweigh student gender-typed orientation. Indeed, given the repeatedly demonstrated variation between different groups of girls within either school sector, studies that do show a school effect must be interpreted with great caution. There are encouraging indications in this literature of the potential for school interventions to counteract some of the typical gender limitations, as well as some indication that the above differences are also weakening in the light of general experience of a world less structured around gender difference.

At this point the discussion turns to an investigation of the research into single-sex education for boys.

Single-sex schools for boys' education

Through the 1990s, the rise of interest in boys' education, which was frequently accompanied by claims of boys' special and different needs, had led to some renewed interest in single-sex education for boys. While much of this interest was concerned with developing single-sex strategies within coeducational schools, there were also some voices promoting the idea of separate schooling for boys. The boys school headmaster quoted in the Introduction appears to adopt the position that boys schools are 'selling out' on their primary role of educating boys which, in his view at least, is markedly different from a general approach to educating young people. But there is no specific identification of exactly what those different approaches entail. While there is a good deal of writing about the putative virtues of boys schools for boys and analyses of the ways in which boys are currently 'missing out', there is little by way of carefully conducted research to sustain these positions. Appeals to history and tradition abound – and yet this sort of nostalgia for earlier times can be no justification for present-day schooling.

The common thread in the rhetoric about boys' educational needs is the theme of difference. Boys, it is repeatedly claimed, are fundamentally different from girls. This claim is frequently made without any basis in evidence – it is offered as a fundamental truth, a statement of such commonsensical veracity that only a fool could doubt. The ready public acceptance of the difference thesis is evidenced by the fact that a book about the issue of raising boys became a long-running bestseller in the Australian book market. Theories about testosterone, the male sex hormone popularly connected to explanations of boys' aggressive behaviour, are cited as indisputable evidence of inevitable behavioural difference. Such theories discount the fact that testosterone is also present in females, albeit generally at lower levels, and, even more importantly that testosterone production has been shown to be consequent upon aggressive activity and not necessarily its antecedent. In other words, it is another version of the chicken and egg problem, with evidence of aggression producing testosterone rather than testosterone producing aggression.

At other times, appeals to biology in terms of brain structures and formation are offered. However, this too cannot be sustained by research evidence. Comprehensive overviews from researchers from fields as diverse as biology, neuroscience, genetics and neuropsychology have investigated these claims and concur in dismissing them in terms of any potential to generalise about sex differences in intellectual functioning (Rogers 1999). And, as noted earlier, frequently the strategies advanced for boys' education appear to commend practices that are also associated with good education for girls!

While there are anecdotal accounts of teachers doing excellent work with boys in boys schools, none of these experiences would have to be limited to single-sex schools. One New South Wales boys school principal, for example, proudly spoke of the success they had experienced in teaching the boys to tap dance (at the time of the film *Tap Dogs*). The teachers involved asserted that this teaching would not have been possible in a mixed environment because of the boys' heightened self-consciousness in the presence of girls. However, this claim was not subject to testing. It may be that the results could have been similar at a mixed school, then again possibly not. In all probability the quality of teaching would have been crucial – but then this is surely the case in just about every educational endeavour.

In 2003 the ACT Council of Parents & Citizens Associations produced a website publication titled *Boys-Only Schooling is Not the Solution*. Their overview of research into issues of boys' schooling led them to reject single-sex schooling and classrooms as outdated and less likely to promote optimal adjustment to life after school. They also note that the research showed some small effect of school gender context but that the effect 'pales into significance' compared with the influence of teacher quality.

The literature on boys and education does not include the wealth of studies of attitudes, enrolments and achievement levels that was covered by the research into girls' education. This lack is somewhat surprising given that, if boys are fundamentally different from girls, it is to be expected that their education would be best delivered in special purpose institutions and this would be demonstrable in terms of school effects. And yet this case has not been strongly advanced, even within the boys schools themselves. Only a very small number of boys schools applied for the government's special grant of $5000 to provide 'lighthouse schools' for boys' education, whereas a large number of coeducational schools at both primary, secondary and combined levels have done so.

Rarely, if at all, does the publicity for the diminishing number of boys schools promote the idea that their high quality education derives from their being boys-only institutions. However, this omission is also evidence of the specific concerns with boys' education noted below.

In general terms, boys from middle-class backgrounds have continued to be successful at their middle-class schools – whether these schools are public or private – and whether they are single-sex or coeducational. It has never been the case that such boys were seen as disadvantaged by standard educational treatments. While the movement for girls and education was able to show how girls were excluded from many areas of normal schooling just because they were girls, this was not and is not the case for boys. In other words, the case for single-sex schools for girls was made by some feminist educators on the basis of research demonstrating that girls typically missed out on opportunities in coeducational schools. Since this time, there has been a widespread adoption of strategies in coeducational schools to overcome barriers to girls' education. Some of these strategies have included the formation of single-sex classes. While there have been reports of some qualified success with this strategy, its usefulness also derives from its novelty and from its capacity to mobilise interest and attention from teachers, parents and other significant people in the girls' life worlds. There have been similarly enthusiastic reports of success with single-sex classrooms for boys education (Townsend 2002). Once again, the level of interest of particular teachers would appear to be heavily implicated in the success of the strategy. This is not to say it is a bad thing for teachers and schools to have attempted. Rather the message is that it cannot be assumed that the single-sex grouping in or of itself is the dependent variable of most significance to the outcomes.

The situation in 2003 in favour of single-sex schooling for girls is not nearly so clear cut as it was some thirty years ago. From the point of view of the boys' education movement, however, the case for separate schooling has not been made.

5

OVERSEAS STUDIES

Overview

This chapter begins with a close examination of the issue of school gender context in terms of the British research, including studies of school effects in Ireland. Following this, some investigations of school gender context in European schooling are examined. The discussion then moves to the situation in North America where there are relatively few single-sex schools and where the issue has only recently begun to arouse debate and increasing interest.

The discussion of the merits of single-sex schooling as compared with coeducation now turns to research studies from overseas. In including overseas work it is first of all important to note that the structures of schooling and the cultural expectations associated with it are significantly different in different places. Just as life for a schoolboy in twenty-first century Australia is markedly different from, say, what it would have been like in nineteenth-century school days, so too will there be entrenched cultural differences between being a girl in contemporary Australia and being a girl in contemporary Indian society. And real differences exist between the way schooling is enacted even within English-speaking countries such as England and the United States. It is indeed dangerous to assume that because single-sex schools work well in one country they will do equally well in other places. And yet, in earlier times (and in some previous research) gender was regarded as a constant across cultures and hence much attention was paid to overseas research on the issue and conclusions urged – in ways that nowadays we would want to question and challenge. At the same time, studies which have looked at the question from their particular cultural vantage points can offer some insights into the ways in which gender becomes re-enacted in schooling. Such work has much potential use in developing an understanding of how things might work in the here and now.

Findings from British research

The initial impetus for raising the question about single-sex schooling as compared with coeducation came from studies of British schooling. In the United Kingdom there is a long-established tradition of single-sex schools, within both the public and private sectors. Compared with the Australian situation, the British private fee-paying schools serve a much smaller social group. The fees associated with these schools are considerably higher than those for comparable Australian schools and hence the dual public/private education system is even more clearly tied to class divisions than in this country. Comparisons across public and private sectors are even more likely to be contaminated by variables such as wealth, social and cultural capital, and so on. Meanwhile, the large numbers within government schooling in both single-sex and mixed schools would appear to provide much more potential for comparative study of the effect of school gender context on educational outcomes. However, the situation is less straightforward than first might appear.

Some of what are now government schools in England were once 'maintained' schools (supported by a benefactor, often a royal one; for example, King Edward VI schools) whose pedigrees date back several hundred years and whose proud traditions of impressive academic achievement are supported by rigorous testing and streaming. The notorious 11+ examination served these schools well. For much of the twentieth century, this examination was undertaken by all school children in the year after they turned 11 and their subsequent schooling was arranged on the basis of their results in this examination. While proportions varied in terms of numbers of places available in different areas, the general rule was that the top 20 per cent of 12-year-olds went on to grammar schools, the next 20 per cent to technical schools and the remaining 60 per cent attended secondary modern schools. While many of the grammar schools were single-sex institutions, the majority of the other schools were mixed. This scheme effected a sort of academic class system within the government schools. The broadly understood pattern was that those who had 'passed the 11+' went to the academic grammar school and the others, who were understood to have 'failed the 11+', took educational paths that rarely led to university or tertiary education.

In the 1970s the Labour government was committed to achieving more equitable educational arrangements. It initiated a campaign dedicated to the establishment of comprehensive schools, which effectively meant the end of the three-tiered system of secondary schooling. This was the period at which Dale's research into the question of mixed or single-sex school was undertaken (Dale 1969, 1971, 1974), against the background of a political move towards comprehensive schools. Dale's conclusions were in line with the political direction of the time.

Educational change rarely comes quickly. The connection between academic excellence and single-sex schooling had been established within the three-tiered system of secondary schooling. While most of the newer British high schools were developed along comprehensive lines, the older ones retained their names, their atmosphere and, in a significant number of cases, their single-sex composition. Thus studies that sought to compare results within the government system were still caught up in the older distinctions. Because of the degree of public concern about the issue of single-sex schooling, especially in the case of girls' education, the government commissioned two large-scale studies in the early 1980s to investigate the question. As noted in the previous chapter, both studies came to the conclusion that the sorts of results achieved by girls at school were not determined by the gender composition of the school but were much more affected by the academic orientation of the school (that is, whether it was a grammar school or not), social background, parental education and measured student ability at entry. By this time Dale had come out in favour of mixed schools and these two large-scale studies had shown that gender context was not a determinant of girls' achievement, but still the question continued to attract debate and research. Undoubtedly at least some of the support for the idea of high achievement being connected to single-sex schools came from those who resisted the government's move to comprehensives in preference for the older, more stringently academic tradition. This position is still being promoted in the literature in favour of retaining both boys schools and girls schools.

Throughout the 1980s a number of other British studies engaged with the question of school gender context as it affected female academic achievement. Many of the themes taken up in this research endeavour were copied by Australian researchers and are among those reported in the previous chapter. To this end, there were analyses of the subject choices of girls in senior school which indicated a greater tendency to polarisation into girls' subjects and boys' subjects in coeducational schools than in single-sex schools; investigations of girls' achievement levels, especially in non-traditional areas such as maths and science, appeared not to be influenced by school gender context. Much of this research was constructed against a considerable background of British studies showing how girls were marginalised in the typical coeducational school experience. For example, girls in mixed classes had been shown to be regarded by teachers as less able than their male peers (Clarricoates 1980). To this end Delamont (1980) had documented cases of 'normal' classroom practice in which there were gender distinctions in teacher expectation and explicit direction, which were subsequently followed by gender conformist behaviour on the part of the students. Spender & Sarah (1980) had identified that in standard classroom treatments boys got three times the amount of teacher attention as did girls. And, perhaps most significantly, Stanworth (1982) had identified gender dimensions of the classroom which meant that girls were rendered invisible. In this study both teachers and male students rarely knew by name numbers of the girls in their classes and dismissed them with the line 'and the rest were girls'.

It is noteworthy that much of this classroom-based research took place in the late 1970s and early 1980s in England. This was a time of considerable energy around questions of gender, and women's liberation was a widely recognised catchcry. The schools at the time most probably reflected a conservative vision of women's place that was transmitted through the unofficial or hidden curriculum to the students. While there was certainly not the same degree of classroom research happening in Australia at the time, the British results received a good deal of publicity in this country as well. And yet the question must be raised as to whether the situation in Australian schools would have been comparable to that found in British ones, given that gender positioning is a key element within cultures and the culture of schooling was different here. For one thing, here in Australia there were not the rigid divisions of students into more and less academic schools from the age of twelve. However, there were, and continue to be, different social codes about when and how to speak, and while Australians will differ dramatically along these lines, they are generally more relaxed about speaking out than the British. Nevertheless, Spender's research (Spender 1982) about girls' losing out in terms of speaking in class was widely accepted to be true of Australian classrooms as well as of the British ones of the original research.

The point for this discussion is that the research into school gender context effects in the United Kingdom was grounded in a good deal of empirical work which showed that girls were routinely disadvantaged in standard schooling practice. They were regarded as inferior students, received less teacher attention, were expected not to achieve highly and so on. It is not surprising that the press for girls-only schooling took on a particular edge. To paraphrase the earlier quotation from Spender (see the Introduction), it was generally thought to be important to establish schools for girls that were consciously dedicated to female achievement in order to redress the systematic anti-female bias within normal schooling. Even Marxist feminists who had vigorously opposed the class-divided educational system and were committed to comprehensivisation were prepared to re-think this commitment in terms of girls' education (Arnot 1983; Deem 1984). The only trouble was that both Dale's research and the two large-scale studies[1] that followed it had not shown girls' academic achievements were lower in coeducation than in single-sex schools, once all the other variables had been taken into account.

Subsequent British studies were more mixed in their findings. Every now and then for the next fifteen years, a study would emerge that showed that girls from single-sex schools were performing at higher levels than those in mixed schools. The question took on some aspects of a forest fire – now you see it, now you don't. With the wisdom of hindsight it can now be said that the degree to which school effects influence student experience and final achievement is evidently extremely complex. Variations could well be in terms of the particular student group, the mix of backgrounds, the cohesiveness of the teaching staff, their level of expertise, the quality of school leadership, the adequacy of school resources, all of which have been shown to impact on student outcomes. Within this complex mix it is virtually impossible to isolate school gender context as a variable – even if that variable is seen as constant across time, a proposition that is highly dubious. Girls schools in 2003 are likely to be very different places from girls schools in 1963 or 1983, but the actual qualitative dimensions of these differences have not been researched. A recent overview of all the British work into school gender context (Elwood & Gipps 1999) was supportive of the 1983 large-scale studies referred to above. It concluded as follows:

- the pattern of difference and similarities in academic performance of girls and boys suggests that the performance of a school in terms of examination results has much less to do with whether it is single-sex or not than with other factors;

- the better performances of girls schools are not strictly related to single-sexness but to differences in intake that relate to social class and ability and the histories and traditions of these schools;
- social class and prior attainment remain the most powerful predictors of educational achievement;
- there are bigger differences between types of school (that is, whether it is independent, selective or comprehensive) than whether it is single-sex or not; and
- certain schools show different selectiveness for certain sub-groups of pupils, with coeducation having a stronger impact on low-ability girls and boys. (Elwood & Gipps 1999, p. 51)

The general conclusion from this review is that there is no conclusive evidence to suggest that single-sex schooling is better than coeducational schooling.

It seems that in Britain the evidence continues to support the broader subject choices of girls at single-sex schools and students from both types of schools share a perception that single-sex schools are more academic whereas coeducational schools are more social. Elwood and Gipps also report continued interest in the idea of single-sex classes for some of the secondary school experience for both girls and boys. Notwithstanding this comprehensive overview, a recent and much publicised report of the NFER (National Foundation for Educational Research) identified certain advantages for students in single-sex schools (Spielhofer et al. 2002). In this study there were performance gains for girls in single-sex comprehensive schools over girls in mixed comprehensive schools, but no gains for either school gender context in the grammar schools. The benefits that were identified appeared to be particularly in favour of girls at the lower end of the ability range. For boys, the effect of attending a single-sex grammar school was associated with higher grades. While the girls from girls schools were seen to be more likely to undertake non-traditional subjects, the boys in the boys schools tended to stay with more traditional male-dominated subject areas when compared with boys in mixed schools. Once again, the results of this study form a mixed bag and one that is less than adequate for the formulation of policy about school gender context.

Meanwhile in Ireland, which operates as a natural laboratory for the question of school gender context, given that its school population appears more evenly spread across the two types of schooling, investigations continue to produce ambivalent results. In a major overview of this work (Hannan et al. 1996) the authors concluded that the academic achievement levels of girls and boys were generally not affected by their attendance at either a coeducational or a single-sex school, although they noted that coeducation appeared to have a depressant effect on the achievement of low-ability girls. These researchers concurred with the idea that there is a great deal of variation between schools on all the indicators of schooling outcomes and suggest that the issue of gender context is less significant than a range of other variables. They share a concern to be found in both the British and Australian work that girls' self-image and levels of self-confidence tend to be lower than those of boys, regardless of school type. A particularly interesting finding to emerge from this Irish study was that boys from coeducational schools tended to have more liberal attitudes than those from single-sex schools – a finding that echoes some of the early Australian work noted previously.

Despite cultural differences, there is a striking degree of similarity in the findings on this question in the British and Irish studies and the Australian research, a perception that reveals some deep cultural thread in Australian schooling which was, as we have seen, modelled on its British antecedents. Moreover, as is the case in Australia, these school systems are structured around a meritocratic model in which success in a particular area at school tends to be the direction of later life choices. Academic achievement is seen as an accumulation of intellectual experience. Similarly, lack of achievement at school can serve as a barrier to future learning. Being seen as 'bright' at school has been shown to have different connotations for girls and boys and these vary in terms of age, school year level and social background. School cultures vary in terms of their academic orientation as well as features such as their gender context, their level of teacher expertise, effective leadership, resource base, to name a few of the more salient. Young people's identities are constructed around these variables. The high flyer in science will be dismissed as 'nerdy' in one school and well respected in another; similarly the bright girl will be seen as a boringly dutiful know-all in one group but highly regarded in another. And while some of these personality traits may be short term, in other cases they can last well into adulthood and affect the individual's choices and life outcomes, which is why the question of the degree to which school gender context affects individual achievement continues to arise. However, despite repeated claims, research has not been able to demonstrate a consistent relationship between schooling culture and school gender context.

Other cultures: similar questions

I have argued earlier in this book that schooling inevitably reflects aspects of the surrounding culture and thus, in this sense, solutions to schooling issues cannot readily be imported across cultures. There are two issues relevant to the current debate. First, the ways in which different cultures operate around gender and the profound differences between cultures in terms of their gender distinction or gender inclusivity means that it is unlikely educational issues around gender will easily translate from one culture to another. Researchers have engaged in comparisons across cultures in terms of sex-segregated schooling, perhaps taking the view that sex is a unilateral given and hence it operates above and beyond culture. Such a position has become increasingly difficult to maintain in the face of the many demonstrations that sex differences are culturally inscribed and take their meaning very differently in different cultures. Secondly, the degree to which schooling matters in terms of its availability, the ways in which it is structured, its content, the accepted pedagogic style and its overall value, are all aspects of cultural difference. Taken together, these features work against the ready assumption that findings from studies of single-sex schools in, say, Nigeria or Thailand or Barbados (these places and many others appear in the literature) compared with coeducation will hold true for the situation in contemporary Australia, even though we have some students from all of these places in our schools. This rationale explains the initial concentration on Australian research in this review, followed by attention to studies from the United Kingdom and North America.

To the extent that European culture, in a broadly Western sense, continues to be somewhat similar to our own, I will make brief mention here of some of the recent European studies which have looked at single-sex schooling. One large study of student 'well-being' investigated over two thousand Belgian upper primary school children and found that, at this level at least, school type (whether it was single-sex or not) did not appear to have an impact on girls' school experience (Brutsauert & Bracke 1994). An interesting feature of this study was that there appeared to be a connection between boys' general sense of well-being and the presence or absence of male teachers, with boys' sense of well-being enhanced when there were at least some male teachers on the staff. Overall, however, neither the boys nor the girls appeared to be affected by the presence or absence of opposite sex students in their classes. A later Belgian study of attitudes of secondary school students (Brutsauert 1999) found that girls in coeducational schools, when compared with girls in single-sex schools, did identify themselves more strongly with feminine traits but also with more masculine ones. In other words these girls exhibited a wider range of personality characteristics, although their classroom behaviour appeared to be 'more inhibited' than that of the girls in single-sex schools.

A recent German study investigated boys' achievements, attitudes and well-being across the two types of school and found that overall the similarities between boys on all these dimensions were far greater than any difference. On the basis of their evidence, the authors proceed to challenge the idea that boys are better off in coeducation (Holz-Ebeling et al. 2000). Another German study revealed that girls who had been taught in single-sex classes in science for one year exhibited more favourable attitudes to science than did those who had experienced only coeducation, whereas boys' attitudes appeared unaffected by either type of class experience (Kessels et al. 2002). A third German study (Rost & Pruisken 2000) investigated academic self-concept, sex-role orientation, leisure interests and motivation across three groups: girls in girls schools; girls in single-sex classes within coeducational schools; and boys in the same coeducational schools. The study did find sex differences along these dimensions – for example, the girls identified different leisure interests from those of the boys – however, these differences were apparent whether or not the students attended a single-sex school.

The view from North America

In North America, school achievement is less tied to post-school paths. For one thing, the rates of school completion are in general much higher than for the United Kingdom or Australia. High school graduation, for those who undertake higher education, is often followed by a broad undergraduate educational experience wherein subjects can be studied 'from scratch' with no assumption of prior learning. In this environment the picture of the successful student is less tightly determined by school experience.

In many respects the question of single-sex schooling presents a different set of issues in North America. Here, the established tradition is one of coeducation which, at least in the United States, is vested with legal authority as the right and proper way for schooling to be organised. This situation reflects the fact that the major equity movements here have centred on issues of race rather than of gender. But there are other differences as well. In England and Australia it is still possible to attend a single-sex school and then to proceed to university, which is organised along coeducational lines albeit with predictable gender imbalance in certain areas. In the United States the vast majority of schools are coeducational, but the higher education institutions have had, up until the recent past, a tradition of some single-sex experience, especially in the case of the prestigious women's colleges on the East Coast. Places such as Smith and Vassar are proudly cited as eminent houses of women's higher learning. The changes that have occurred in recent decades in terms of some of these institutions becoming coeducational have been the source of considerable lament and critique in American educational circles.

Unlike the situation in Britain and Australia, there was little research through the 1980s around the question of gender equity in education. To an outsider, it appeared as though the long-lasting Reagan regime had effectively stifled debates around gender equity in favour of a notional complementarity of men and women in all aspects of life and work. However, in the early 1990s several publications were released which echoed the outrage and deeply felt sense of injustice that had coloured earlier reports here and in the United Kingdom. Possibly most notable was M. and D. Sadkers' 1994 work: *Failing at Fairness: How America's Schools Cheat Girls*, the title of which conveys the authors' position fairly accurately. In ways highly reminiscent of the earlier Australian and British work, the Sadkers' book presents comprehensive and detailed evidence of schooling practices in which girls are treated as second-class citizens. This book appeared shortly after the publication of a report from the American Association of University Women (AAUW) titled *How Schools Shortchange Girls* (1992), which found that girls were disadvantaged in classrooms by being called on less frequently and encouraged less than male students. In a subsequent report the AAUW noted 'Single-sex programs deserve consideration as a vehicle to address specific needs or remedy existing inequities' (Hansen et al. 1995, p. 60). The stage was set for an investigation into the possibilities offered by single-sex institutions.

Despite the fact that it was an American, James Coleman, who, back in 1966, proffered the suggestion that the 'dating and rating' atmosphere of American high schools would counteract the development of intellectual endeavour as an appropriate goal of schooling, American research on the question of school gender context has been pursued only very recently, much more recently than in Australia and Britain. Because of the overwhelming adoption of coeducation in American schooling practice, any examination of single-sex schooling has, until very recently, had to concentrate on schools outside the standard educational provision. The Catholic school system in North America has been the location of a good deal of the recent research into the question of school gender context. Although the system of Catholic schooling is not as established as in Australia, there are sufficient numbers of Catholic schools to undertake comparative studies. Many of these schools are single-sex.

Overall, the American work tends to be more inclined to conclude that single-sex schooling is associated with higher academic achievement, especially in the case of girls. An early study into Catholic schools had found that 'single-sex schools appear to deliver specific advantages to their students. The results are particularly strong for girls' schools' (Lee & Bryk 1986, p. 394). In a special report published in 1992, the US Department of Education concluded that 'there is empirical support for the view that single-sex schools may accrue positive outcomes, particularly for young women' (US Department of Education 1992, p. 35). A recent overview of research in the area concluded that 'the predominance of research certainly shows a role for single-sex schools (as an option if not a norm)' (Mael 1998, p. 12). A subsequent AAUW report, while overall somewhat critical of seeing single-sex schools as a solution, noted: 'There is something of a consensus that girls in single-sex schools tend to perceive subjects such as math and physics as less "masculine" and may have stronger preferences for them than their coeducated peers' (Haag 1998, p. 18).

Meanwhile, one of the most prolific American researchers in this area, Cornelius Riordan, who initially appeared to be making the case for the superiority of single-sex schooling for all students, has most recently refined his analysis. Having described the whole area as 'over-politicised and underresearched', Riordan now concludes that single-sex schools do not greatly influence the academic achievement of advantaged students, but they do so for disadvantaged students. His view is clearly put in the following:

> The academic and developmental consequences of attending one type of school versus another type of school are virtually zero for middle class and otherwise advantaged students; by contrast, the consequences are significant for students who are or have been historically or traditionally disadvantaged – minorities, low and working-class youth, and females (so long as the females are not affluent). (Riordan 1998, p. 53)

Elsewhere Riordan insists that the academic culture associated with single-sex schooling cannot be produced by having one or two single-sex classrooms. For him the gender context of the whole institution has to be either single-sex or coeducational as he sees the institutional culture of the whole as the important variable.

One of the difficulties for American studies of single-sex schooling has traditionally been that schools are required by law not to discriminate on all the usual grounds, which of course include sex. Only very recently (May 2002), the federal government of the United States issued new regulations providing for some flexibility in this area and it is anticipated that there will be some ongoing experimentation with single-sex schooling in the public sector. However, the state of California was sufficiently persuaded of the potential benefits of single-sex schooling that in 1998 it initiated a trial of single-sex schools in six districts. Despite some early success with the establishment of the new academies, for which there were associated financial incentives, after two or three years only one remained open (Hubbard & Datnow 2002). In other words, this trial echoed findings in both Australia and Britain with single-sex classes, namely that unless there is commitment from all involved – teachers, students, parents and school community – the experiment is unlikely to succeed. In other areas similar trials of single-sex schooling are ongoing.

It would be wrong to assume that all American research comes down in favour of single-sex schooling. In 1994, researchers Lee and Marks found that sex stereotyping occurs equally as much in single-sex schools as in coeducational ones, although the forms it takes may be different (Lee & Marks 1994). This study, which included boys-only schools, coeducational schools and girls-only schools, found incidences of 'gender reinforcement and embedded discrimination in all types of schools', and these features were more common in single-sex schools. However, the authors noted that active discrimination against females as females, regardless of gender conformity, can only occur in a situation in which both sexes are present.

In general, it seems as though there is some popular support for the notion of single-sex schooling in the United States, despite the lack of overwhelming empirical evidence to sustain the position. The respected AAUW (American Association of University Women) published a report in 1998 entitled *Separated by Sex: A Critical Look at Single-sex Education for Girls*, in which the authors note the lack of consistency in the research results and the small amount of research generally in

America on this topic. They note: 'Myth and popular notions, however, seem to be mixed up with what is actually known from research about the efficacy of single-sex classes compared to coed ones' (Campbell & Wahl 1998). This suggestion alerts readers to the position that combinations of myth and popular notions appear recurrently through discussions of the effects of school gender context in general and single-sex schools in particular.

Conclusions

As seen in similar studies in Australia and the United Kingdom, American researchers have identified data showing girls' achievement levels at single-sex schools to be ahead of those in coeducational schools, but once the findings are adjusted for socioeconomic or ability variables, these differences either notably diminish or disappear completely.

It is certainly true that the outrage that was expressed in Australia and Britain about the plight of girls in education was not expressed in the United States until considerably later. Hence it is possible that the appeal of the single-sex solution will prove to be a short-lived phenomenon. Again, it may be a temporary strategy to alert educators to some of the negative effects of gender typing and harassment shown to operate in some mixed classes and schools.

As we have seen earlier in the debate, there are some voices from feminist educators who see two sides of the coin insofar as single-sex schools and classrooms may be adopted as a solution to the problem of gender limitations, but they also have the potential to work against the best interests of students. In the words of one European commentator:

> Sex segregated education can be used for emancipation or oppression. As a method, it does not guarantee an outcome. The intentions, the understanding of people, and their gender, the pedagogical attitudes and practices, are crucial, as in all pedagogical work. (Kruse 1996, p. 189)

Meanwhile, there are interesting similarities between some of the findings from Britain and North America in terms of the Australian situation. Despite acknowledged differences in the ways in which schools are structured, researchers have experienced the same difficulties in attempting to resolve the question: Which is the best way to school? This outcome suggests both the complexity of the issues involved and the difficulties faced by researchers in their effort to overcome them. At the same time, research on this question raises more issues and provokes insights about the whole project of schooling and the ways in which it is organised. Perhaps the most crucial insight to come from the overseas work concerns the recent American finding in favour of single-sex schools for students from disadvantaged backgrounds (Riordan 2002), a position which is echoed in the recent British work (Spielhofer 2002). In Australia to date, there has not been research which looks specifically at the ways in which single-sex schooling might operate for underprivileged youth, although there have been hints of connections as early as Carpenter (1985). To some extent, given the demise of single-sex schools within most state government school systems, it may not be possible to conduct this research. However, the overseas work indicates an interesting interaction between socioeconomic level and school gender context which should not be overlooked.

6

REACHING TOWARDS CONCLUSIONS

Overview
In this chapter themes from the previous chapters are drawn together in terms of what can be said about the question of school gender context and what has been learnt about education in general in the effort to promote gender equity.

Questions about the relative merits of single-sex schooling as compared with coeducation are still with us, although the ways in which they are framed have become much more nuanced. There is no conclusive answer for all young people, much less all girls or all boys, even at this particular historical moment – but perhaps such an answer is no longer to be expected. Given the lack of closure in the reported research on this issue, it is perhaps ridiculously optimistic to attempt to reach any conclusions at all. And yet, as I shall attempt to show in these few pages, I believe there are things that can reliably be said about schooling in terms of gender context. Even more profitably, there are features that have been revealed about the whole ambit of educational endeavour through raising the question about schooling style and structure.

Complexity of schooling revealed
First, the very complexity of the practice of schooling has been revealed. Most schools in Australia typically serve a range of student backgrounds and potentials. Their students come from backgrounds that differ significantly in terms of wealth, ethnicity, race, parental education, religious affiliation, geographic location and so on. There are clear

differences between students in all of these features, as well as in intellectual capacity, personal development and gender. Schools themselves differ in terms of external variables, such as the communities they serve and the degree of homogeneity within their own community. Differences between schools also involve aspects of size, the range of school years they encompass, the size of their classes, their locations, their level of resources, their participation in either the government or non-government system and so on. Internal qualitative variables may be even more important in their capacity to affect the quality of school experience. These differences include the quality of leadership in the school, the range of experience and expertise among the teachers, the level of engagement of teachers and school leaders, the involvement of the parent community – all of which are much more difficult to measure and assign a value to than the earlier variables. Given this range of potential complexity, it is not surprising that studies which home in on one feature, namely whether the school is single-sex or not, have not been able to demonstrate consistent effects. The point was made most forcefully by some American researchers:

> While the question 'Are single-sex classes better than coed classes?' may sound logical, it makes little sense when there is no consideration of what goes on in the classes, the pedagogy and practice of the teachers, or anything about the students other than their sex. Yet the public, the media, educators and even some researchers compare classes and attribute outcomes to this single factor of whether the class is all girls, all boys or girls and boys together. (Campbell & Wahl 1998, p. 63)

As noted in an earlier chapter, schooling as we know it took its shape from the single-sex boys schools of earlier times. By 2003 all of our social institutions, including schooling, have undergone considerable change. Given that many social demarcations pertaining to gender have become thoroughly outmoded, it is rather curious that the question of single-sex schooling has persisted as long as it has.

Perhaps one reason for this relates to the paradoxical nature of contemporary schooling. The local school, that ubiquitous presence in the neighbourhood, still, in many respects, operates as a closed institution whose rules and processes are known only to insiders. Despite the fact that most adults have had some experience of school-based education, schooling is still a rather private and mysterious business. Recently there has been a considerable amount of rhetoric about school choice and the importance of finding out about a school before committing one's son or daughter to spending a good deal of their time there. And yet it is notoriously difficult to access this 'insider' knowledge. In addition, there is the further complication that schools may change radically when particular teachers leave or school leaders move. Most people, parents and teachers, register the difficulty of finding out what is really going on inside the black box of schooling. At the same time, one single feature, the school's gender composition, is usually immediately evident, even to the casual viewer. Perhaps the very availability of this piece of knowledge about the school has added to its being seen as particularly significant in educational outcomes. The myths and popular notions about the virtue of single-sex schooling may stem in part from this most obvious distinction between schools, together with the relative rarity of such schools within the current provision.

Of course the trouble with myths around social institutions such as schooling is that they can readily become self-fulfilling prophecies. The availability of raw data showing girls' performance to be better in single-sex schools serves to build credibility in the thesis that such schools deliver a better education in terms of academic achievement than do coeducational ones. However, as has been repeatedly seen in the studies reported in this book, careful analysis reveals that nearly always the better results can be explained by differences in some combination of measured ability and family background, rather than being due to the school's gender context. In addition to which, given the increased number of coeducational schools serving middle-class communities, the supposed advantage is not nearly so evident as once it was. Unfortunately myths and popular notions are rarely amenable to the logic of scientific reasoning, at least in the first instance. The issue of girls' superior academic performance being accountable by attendance at a girls-only school may be, by 2004, just such a popular notion whose shelf life has extended beyond its usefulness and validity.

Girls' academic capacity revealed

The press for girls' education arose from a sense that girls were typically not being afforded the same degree of educational opportunity as boys. The attention to single-sex schools and classes grew out of the desire to ensure that girls were given those opportunities. It seems fairly obvious that segregated schools for girls were necessary during a time when there was a high level of entrenched gender segregation in the wider society. At times when women were not admitted to university, had to struggle over the right to vote, could not own property, were not permitted to inherit the family estates, had very limited career opportunities, were not allowed to take out a bank loan, nor to enter a range of exclusive men's clubs and other venues, the chances of girls being afforded an equal educational experience to boys at mixed schools would have been remote. There can be no doubt that in the recent past, single-sex schools for girls played a significant role in demonstrating female capacity for academic achievement and in providing spaces where that achievement could be fostered. The question now becomes whether they continue to be necessary for female intellectual development. And, as we have seen, the evidence is highly inconclusive.

The recent publicity about girls 'dominating' and 'outperforming' boys may do more to destabilise the sense of female achievement needing a protected, safe, all-female environment than anything else to date. The boys and education lobby has provoked a good deal of the recent publicity about female academic achievement and it is evident that many girls from the coeducational schools are doing very well in the end of school examinations. The case for girls needing a single-sex environment in order to achieve academically is now on shaky ground indeed.

Gender has become a high-profile issue in schools

Furthermore, as a result of the considerable publicity around gender and schooling over the last twenty years, teachers in coeducational schools have become more aware of gender-related behavioural differences in classroom treatments. Similarly, they have become much more aware of ways of managing disruptive behaviour, of issues around sexual harassment, of the need to encourage both boys and girls in non-traditional areas. And the young people themselves are also much more conscious of gender issues and willing to engage in debates about fairness and equity on their own behalf as well as on behalf of others. In other words, gender has become a much more visible feature in coeducational classrooms around the country. As some would have it, gender has been 'mainstreamed' in education. Consequently, pedagogies have been developed, and continue to be developed, which challenge gender-based limitations and address gender-based differences in classroom behaviours.

In this environment it was perhaps not surprising that initiatives to provide girls with single-sex classrooms in some subject areas, notably science and maths, were associated with an improvement in girls' achievement levels. In general, however, these results have tended not to be long term. A side effect of such interventions, and one of concern to some feminist educators, was that the initiative itself appeared to imply that girls were incapable in these important learning areas unless they had the opportunity provided by the special environment of the all-girls class. Another criticism was that these strategies did not challenge the boys and their teachers to become more inclusive. Such responses underscore the need for a fully developed model of gender reform in schools, one that involves details of particular stages along the way, rather than the idea that one specific strategy will remedy the whole system.

Trying out single-sex classrooms for boys

Amid the lists of strategies embraced by people concerned with boys' education, there have also been some experiments with single-sex classrooms for boys. These are often led by enthusiastic male teachers who write in glowing terms about the potential of such arrangements to redefine boys' educational experience (Lillico 2002; Townsend 2002). While preliminary results appear very positive, it seems likely that this success will also be short term rather than long term. The experience of single-sex classes for girls showed that the presence of a supportive community of teachers, parents and the students themselves was an essential part of the success of these initiatives. Once again, the lesson here appears to be not so much in terms of the particular gender context, but rather of having energetic and enthusiastic teachers, along with parents and the whole school community committed to the principles of gender equity and the fulfilment of individual potential, working together to that end. If having single-sex classes emerges as a useful device for securing that commitment, then it is surely worth considering, but the results must not be read as having been directly caused by the single-sex context on its own.

Single-sex schooling: a complicated issue

While some single-sex experience within the coeducational school can usually be arranged without too much disturbance and could well emerge as one among the many useful strategies that school communities may choose to employ in the interests of promoting gender equity, the issue of single-sex schools is more complicated. As we have seen, the girls schools can no longer rest on assumptions about their environment being uniquely connected to female academic achievement. The boys schools have only rarely promoted the idea that their environment is specifically suited to boys' learning, tending to rest on their strong traditions and connections with outstanding success in the post-school world. Of course, these success stories could well be ascribed to the privileged class location of the students rather than to particular features of the school. Elite single-sex schools, even those bolstered by long tradition, cannot claim that their schools are uniquely necessary for high achievement by either girls or boys. The task for these schools becomes one of promoting their institutions on other grounds to do with quality of school life, opportunities for personal development and preparation for future careers – features that are much harder to demonstrate in quantifiable concrete terms. This job becomes even more difficult in the face of evidence that students tend to see the environment of the mixed school as more sociable while they see the single-sex school as more academic. Meanwhile, the increasing tendency for former boys schools to adopt coeducation may be seen as reflecting public opinion that coeducational environments offer more possibilities for learning how to relate to others, an area seen as particularly important in a society that increasingly turns on information and communication.

In Australia, the single-sex schools are generally non-government schools, by and large associated with social and economic advantage, when compared with the majority of students in coeducational public schools. Research into the effect of school gender context in this country repeatedly identified the difficulty of separating the interacting effects of social background and school organisation on educational outcomes. This research also failed to indicate a consistent connection between attendance at these schools and educational achievement, so long as other effects were taken into account. Researchers repeatedly found no clear overall advantage due to the single-sex school context.

A recent finding that has emerged from research in both the United Kingdom and the United States, and which echoes one of the findings of the early Australian study by Carpenter (1985), has been that there do appear to be advantages in terms of educational achievement for some students in single-sex schools. These students, both boys and girls, have been seen to come from disadvantaged social groups. Now, given that such groups comprise an element in the Australian population least likely to be able to attend single-sex schools, this finding presents as a conundrum. It would seem that Australian single-sex schooling is designed to serve the section of the community for whom school gender context makes the least difference, while those who could possibly benefit are denied the experience. The challenge for Australian schooling must be to conduct locally based research into this connection and, if it is seen to apply in a similar way to Australian students, to provide the single-sex school option for a targeted group within the population as a whole.

Alternatively, the challenge would be to identify aspects of the single-sex school experience which could be incorporated into coeducational schools – in the sense of learning from each other as originally put forward by the Commonwealth Schools Commission. However, this strategy would fly in the face of Riordan's (1998) insistence that it was the quality of the whole school that was at issue here, not simply classes within it. Without further research, these claims will remain untested in Australian school environments.

Moving forward

It seems that schooling does still use the rear vision mirror more than is perhaps advisable. Looking at where we have come from, in terms of schooling organisation, may not always provide the best basis for moving forward. The historical opposition between male and female that emerged in many of our social arrangements became reified in schooling to produce separate spheres and species-specific distinctions between girls and boys, men and women. Single-sex schools, at a superficial level, could appear to be the most obvious case of gender difference in schooling treatments. However, as we have seen, the girls schools at least have mounted the case that their environments were necessary to promote girls' learning so that their graduates could move forward and take up public roles in a more liberated time. Certainly the research literature continues to suggest that many girls in such schools often exhibit attitudes less constrained by gender limitation when compared with girls from mixed schools, even though these findings are also in line with the different social class positions of the girls concerned. The case for the boys schools is less promising, in that elite boys schools have not been associated with progressive social attitudes. There are clear implications for all such schools to constantly monitor the degree of fit between the privileges of their student communities and their future membership in a diverse, vibrant and changing culture such as that of contemporary Australia.

One American technique for gearing thinking in terms of reform without getting bogged down in the problems of the present has been to project one's imagination into the future, say ten or twenty years from now. The task then becomes one of describing the ideal world of this imaginary future time and identifying how previous problems were overcome. If we can look towards a world no longer coloured by deep gender distinction in terms of who does what sort of work, wields what sort of political power, earns significant amounts of money, is accorded respect for work done in both the private and the public sphere, then the question of single-sex schooling becomes irrelevant.

Of course there may well be other features of schooling to be debated in terms of the best environments for our young people to grow and prosper. Maybe the K–12 school will replace the primary/secondary divisions, possibly the middle school will be a stand alone institution or the senior school may be more interconnected with TAFE and university than is currently the case. In looking at research around school gender context, this work has limited itself to one dimension within a large range of factors of school organisation. While the Australian society of fifty years ago may have seen schooling separated by sex as the proper means of educating young people, it seems extremely doubtful that a similar belief will be held by subsequent generations.

In the wonderful diversity that is Australia in the twenty-first century, the issue of separate schooling for girls and boys presents as somewhat of an anachronism. And yet, as we have seen, there are a number of valid reasons for looking at it carefully. Our shared interest is in building the sort of society we all want, one in which women and men are free to pursue their callings and for their children to be free to prepare themselves and discover their talents and predilections in environments that are safe, harassment free and conducive to learning. Given the material that has been presented here, it may be that we need to retain some single-sex schools as possibilities for some girls to grow into their potential as fulfilled women in the world. There may be an even stronger case for instituting some single-sex schools in areas of social disadvantage, in order to better assist young people to make their way in a world in which they start unequally prepared. It would also seem to be equally important that the remaining established boys schools take notice of the significant changes in the workplace relating to gender. These issues need to be addressed in their programs if their students are to develop into the sort of participatory and inclusive citizenry that is the hallmark of a truly democratic society.

The overwhelming message to emerge from the research literature reviewed here concerns the importance of schools and teachers being prepared to confront gender limitation in the effort to provide the best of educational experiences for their students, wherever they are at school. Threaded through the studies of school gender context comes the repeated claim that the quality of teaching in the context of a supportive school environment is by far the most important variable affecting student life, personal development and achievement outcomes. There are many elements to be drawn from the research on single-sex education as compared with coeducation that are relevant when considering good teaching. Teachers who are conscious of the gender effects of schooling practice, who are sensitive to issues of student self-esteem, who are prepared to challenge students to rethink their accepted worldviews and gender stereotypes are creating opportunities for young people to develop critical awareness and to think for themselves. Fundamentally then, the question of school gender context returns us to the need for programs in teacher education and teacher professional development to address questions of gender equity in their ongoing analyses of how best to answer the enduring question set by the famous educational philosopher, Jerome Bruner: What shall we teach and to what end?

POSTSCRIPT:
A word about research

To paraphrase the jest that the only sure things in life are death and taxes, I would add – that the question of single-sex schooling versus coeducation will continue to generate ongoing debate in educational circles. It is a topic that arouses speeches full of passionate conviction, illustrative anecdote and personal history. While nearly everybody has an opinion, few can claim to know the answer – at least in ways that can be empirically demonstrated. How could you prove that one form of education was better than the other? From the research reviewed here, this challenge has clearly inspired a wide range of educational studies across different cultures, contexts and at different times. And while it might be simple to demonstrate that prior to 1950 in Australia high academic achievement was closely associated with attendance at a single-sex school, that connection is much more difficult to show in terms of recent schooling outcomes.

In looking at the issue closely it seems one must also ask: Is this a question that it is possible to answer? For whom? And while each of us may have our own personal responses in terms of our own experience and our estimations of the current social conditions operating around gender, it may not be possible to answer for all young people in all schools, much less at all times and across all cultures.

One reason for my own ongoing fascination with the research which has attempted to answer questions about the best way to organise schooling – coeducation or single sex - relates to the fact that in raising the question and considering possible research approaches one has to also learn a good deal about the possibilities and limitations of empirical inquiry in education.

From the outset, there is the question of evidence. What means are there to demonstrate the superiority of one or other type of schooling? Not surprisingly, many researchers immediately look at schooling outcomes in terms of examination results. This does not mean these researchers believe that everything you can say about schooling is revealed by examination scores. Nor would they want to argue that examination scores are the only variable of importance in educational experience. However, academic results provide a sort of concrete evidence that is readily available, especially in Australia in terms of tertiary entrance rankings. In addition, these results are presented in numerical terms that can then be analysed through statistical manipulation. And so researchers can ask questions of the data such as: Is there a correlation between attendance at a single-sex school and high achievement? Is the correlation equally strong for males and females? Do the student scores vary in terms of particular subjects? In this way a picture is built up of schooling outcomes based on the results of examinations. However, it is also important to remember that basic rule: correlation does not imply causation. For example, the fact that student scores of girls at single-sex schools may be higher than those at coeducational schools cannot be taken to imply that it is simply this one feature of their schooling which has produced the better results. Time and again researchers whose work has been reported here have demonstrated that when their analysis involves 'controlling' for other variables this relationship frequently disappears. Hence they argue that it is other features of the particular student groups being compared such as their ability levels, their socioeconomic background, the academic orientation of the school and so on which has led to the better scores.

Certainly the statistical analyses have become ever more complex around this question. These chapters have repeatedly noted the interactions between different variables that impact on student achievement. Statistical analysis not only allows those variables to be quantified and controlled but also inspects the effects of interactions between them. Many of the studies mentioned earlier have adopted HLM (hierarchical linear modelling) in order to be able to speak about which variables are implicated as well as to comment on the degree to which each is involved. An unfortunate side effect of the increasingly sophisticated statistical manipulations associated with this question is that the research seems to get further and further away from the raw data, let alone being indicative of what the actual student school experience is like. And this latter feature – the quality of the school experience – is what many parents, teachers and students themselves want to know about the schools they are considering.

While most would agree that examination results are far from the whole story to be told about the quality of school life, nor are they entirely irrelevant – as any short discussion with parents, teachers and the students themselves will quickly reveal. At the same time, there are lively challenges to this line of research, claiming that it does not reveal what is really going on. What is a particular school like? Are the teachers encouraged to develop pastoral expertise as well as excellence in their particular subjects or year level? Is there strong effective leadership in the school? What is the gender breakdown of the teaching staff? Does the school encourage students to engage in creative endeavours both within and beyond traditional curricula? As we have seen, answers to these questions and many more will impact on the ways in which students grow in their understanding of themselves and their worlds in terms of gender. Traditionally schooling was constrained by notions of gender as limiting the range of possibilities for both girls and boys. Nowadays, young people are unlikely to conform to the rigid prescriptions of former times. However, they still need assistance from teachers and schooling to grow in confidence and self-awareness in order to participate in the post-school world as productive citizens.

Some of the other studies mentioned here – those relating to subject choice, self-esteem levels, attitudes to school and particular subjects, and post-school aspirations – endeavour to make comment about the quality of school life in terms of the ways in which students are encouraged to develop a sense of their own capacities and to follow through with their own choices. Once again, these studies are usually undertaken in terms of large-scale surveys. Given the difficulties of finding consistency in the data, researchers tend to hope that large numbers of responses will produce evidence of a direction when close-grained analyses of a smaller number of students might not. Thus a survey of 1000 students may appear more compelling than an indepth analysis of one or two classes involving just sixty students. However, all such survey work depends on a number of imponderables – for instance the degree to which the respondents have accurate self-knowledge and feel comfortable identifying their positions on an anonymous survey form. Given that we are talking about young people, often still in the process of becoming self-aware and assured adults, these are important issues. Once again the degree of irresolution in the results of this work is not altogether surprising.

There can be no doubt that useful knowledge has been produced about schools from the range of ways in which researchers have addressed the question of school gender context. At the same time, there are real limitations in terms of the adequacy of the measures to generate accounts of the quality of school experience at any one particular site. Close-grained ethnographic style inquiry may produce the desired qualitative description, but that too will be limited in the conclusions that can be drawn being all too specific to the particular site of inquiry. An excellent study of one school that offers great detail about the way in which it is organised around gender may produce knowledge about how that place works, but this knowledge may not be transferable to other school locations.

The only way that one can achieve a more comprehensive picture of what is going on is through some combination of all these empirical approaches in concert with theoretical accounts of the ways in which gender works in terms of social interaction and institutional positioning. Such accounts engage with questions of power as a central issue and offer explanations of, for example, why some boys seek to claim centre stage in terms of classroom disruption and why some girls let them.

And so it seems to me, after reviewing a good deal of the studies of the effect of school gender context, that empirical inquiry will always be limited in its capacity to address this question. To some degree this perception is produced by the terms of the question itself. It presents as an empirical question and most of the attempts to address it have been couched in empirical methodologies. However, as I have attempted to demonstrate in this book, the question is in fact a deeply philosophical one, in that in addressing it one is required to ask other questions about the meaning of education, its value in personal and public terms and the sort of society into which young graduates will enter.

NOTES

Chapter 1
Why are our schools the way they are?

1 Ironically of course these were not 'public' schools at all, but were funded by a mix of private endowment and high fees, catering to the elite.

2 The system of Catholic schools, which sits between these two on most dimensions, was to boom during the second half of the twentieth century with the large numbers of immigrant families from Southern Europe. Catholic schools involved issues to be found in both the state and non-government school systems.

3 Ironically these early women graduates were well represented in the fields of science and medicine, due to the fact that Greek was a university requirement for students in the arts and humanities and at the time Greek was not offered at girls schools because the sexual explicitness of much classical allegory was judged to be inappropriate for young female minds (Miller 1986).

Chapter 2
Girls and education: Gender enters the educational agenda

1 This regulation was terminated at different times in different states, for example New South Wales 1947, Victoria 1969, South Australia 1973. Women were able to be re-employed following marriage but were required to recommence their term of service, hence losing continuity of service and seniority.

2 For an overview of this work see Gill (1987) and Howard (1998).

Chapter 3
Boys' education: Questions of fact and rhetoric

1 Note that this figure is calculated as a percentage of the age cohort who are actively seeking work – thus those who remain in school do not appear.

2   *Boys: Getting it Right: Inquiry into the Education of Boys,* House of Representatives Standing Committee on Education and Training; *Improving Educational Outcomes of Boys,* ACT Department of Education, Youth and Family Services; *The Challenges and Dilemmas Facing Boys in Education Today,* Tasmanian Education Department.

Chapter 4
Single-sex solutions?

1   In a later paper Dale (1975) speculated: 'Maybe nature intended man to be the leader and woman to provide the stability ...' Little wonder his conclusions were attacked by feminists!
2   The Hawthorne effect is a term coined from an American study that showed that when people know they're being measured, they modify their behaviour.

Chapter 5
Overseas studies

1   Bone (1983) and Steedman (1983).

REFERENCES

ACT Council of Parents' & Citizens' Associations (2003), *Boys-only Schooling is Not the Solution*, available at <http://www.schoolparents.canberra. net.au/boy's_education.html>

Ainley, J. & MacKenzie, P. (1999), 'The influence of school factors on young adult life' in *Australia's Young Adults: The Deepening Divide*, Dusseldorp Skills Forum, Sydney, pp. 105–16.

Ainley, J & Daly, P. (2002), 'Participation in science courses in the final year of high school in Australia: The influence of single-sex and coeducational schools' in Datnow, A. & Hubbard, L. (eds), *Gender in Policy and Practice: Perspectives on Single-sex and Coeducational Schooling*, RoutledgeFalmer, London.

American Association of University Women (AAUW) (1992), *How Schools Shortchange Girls*, AAUW Educational Foundation/National Education Foundation, Washington DC.

American Association of University Women (AAUW) (1998), *Separated by Sex: A Critical Look at Single-sex Education for Girls*, AAUW Educational Foundation/National Education Foundation, Washington DC.

Arnot, M. (1983), 'A cloud over cooeducation: An analysis of the forms of transmission of class and gender relations' in Walker, S. & Barton, L. (eds), *Gender, Class and Education*, Falmer, London.

Australian Bureau of Statistics (ABS) (1997), *Australian Social Trends*, Australian Government Printing Service, Canberra.

Baldwin, G. (1990a), 'Gender roles in education: Who is missing out?', *HERDSA News*, vol. 12, no. 2, pp. 10–13.

Baldwin, G. (1990b), 'Single-sex schooling and subject choice: pattern of enrolment at Monash University', *Australian Educational Researcher*, vol. 17, no. 3, pp. 47–64.

Ballenden, C., Davidson, M. & Newell, F. (1984), *Better Chances for Girls: A Handbook of Equal Opportunity Strategies for Use in Schools*, Victorian Institute for Secondary Education, Melbourne.

Bandura, A. (1986), *Social Foundations of Thought and Action: A Social Cognitive Theory*, Prentice-Hall, Englewood Cliffs, New Jersey.

Barboza, E. (1983), Coeducation versus single-sex: Girls' intentions to elect mathematics in senior secondary school, Paper presented at the 53rd Conference of the Australia and New Zealand Association for the Advancement of Science (ANZAAS), Perth.

Beck, J. (1998), *Morality and Citizenship in Education*, Cassell, London.

Bernard, M. (1979), 'Does sex role behaviour influence the way teachers evaluate students?', *Journal of Educational Psychology*, vol. 74, no. 4, pp. 553–62.

Block, J. (1984), *Sex Role Identity and Ego Development*, Jossey-Bass, San Francisco.

Bone, A. (1983), *Girls and Girls Only Schools: A Review of the Evidence*, Equal Opportunities Commission, Manchester, United Kingdom.

Bornholt, L. (1991), Perceptions of achievement in high school maths and English: Multiple sources and multiple dimensions, Unpublished PhD thesis, Macquarie University.

Browne, R. & Fletcher, R. (eds) (1995), *Boys in Schools: Addressing the Real Issues – Behaviour, Values and Relationships*, Finch Publishing, Sydney.

Brutsauert, H. & Bracke, P. (1994), 'Gender context in elementary school', *Educational Studies*, vol. 20, no. 1, pp. 3–10.

Brutsauert, H. (1999), 'Coeducation and gender identity formation: A comparative analysis of secondary schools in Belgium', *British Journal of Sociology of Education*, vol. 20, no. 3, pp. 343–53.

Campbell, P. & Wahl, E. (1998), 'What's sex got to do with it? Simplistic questions, complex answers' in *Separated by Sex: A Critical Look at Single-sex Education for Girls*, AAUW Education Foundation/National Education Foundation, Washington DC, pp. 63–74.

Carpenter, P. (1985), 'Single-sex schooling and girls' academic achievements', *Australian and New Zealand Journal of Sociology*, vol. 21, no. 3, pp. 456–72.

Clark, M. (1989), *The Great Divide: The Construction of Gender in the Primary School*, Curriculum Corporation, Carlton South, Victoria.

Clarricoates, K. (1980), 'The importance of being Earnest … Emma … Tom … Jane: The perception and categorisation of gender conformity and gender deviation in primary schools' in Deem, R. *Schooling for Women's Work*, Routledge & Kegan Paul, London.

Collins, C. (2000), Understanding the relationship between schooling, gender and labour market entry, Paper presented at the conference titled *Educational Attainment and Labour Market Outcomes*, Department of Education, Training and Youth Affairs, Melbourne.

Collins, C., Batten, M., Ainley, J. & Getty, C. (1996), *Gender and School Education*, A project funded by the Commonwealth Department of Employment, Education and Youth Affairs, Australian Government Printing Service, Canberra.

Commonwealth Schools Commission (1975), *Girls, School and Society: Report of the Interim Committee*, Australian Government Printing Service, Canberra.

Commonwealth Schools Commission (1984), *Girls and Tomorrow: The Challenge for Schools*, Australian Government Printing Service, Canberra.

Commonwealth Schools Commission (1987), *The National Policy for the Education of Girls in Australian Schools*, Australian Government Printing Service, Canberra.

Connell, R. W., Ashenden, D., Dowsett, G. & Kessler, S. (1982), *Making the Difference: Schools, Families and Social Division*, Allen & Unwin, Sydney.

Cowell, B. (1981), 'Mixed and single-sex grouping in secondary schools', *Oxford Review of Education*, vol. 7, no. 2, pp. 165–72.

Cox, E. (1995), Boys and girls and the costs of gendered behaviour, Keynote address at the *Promoting Gender Equity Conference*, Canberra, February 22–24.

Dale, R. R. (1969, 1971, 1974), *Mixed or Single-sex School?*, vols I, II and III, Routledge & Kegan Paul, London.
Dale, R. R. (1975), 'Education and sex roles', *Educational Review*, vol. 27, no. 3, pp. 240–48.
Datnow, A. & Hubbard, L. (eds) (2002), *Gender in Policy and Practice: Perspectives on Single-sex and Coeducational Schooling*, RoutledgeFalmer, London.
Davies, B. (1989), *Frogs and Snails and Feminist Tales: Pre-school Children and Gender*, Allen & Unwin, Sydney.
Dawson, C. (1981), Gender differences in preferred science options at the end of primary school, Paper presented at the Department of Education, University of Adelaide.
Deem, R. (1984), *Co-Education Reconsidered*, Open University Press, Milton Keynes, United Kingdom.
Delamont, S. (1980), *Sex Roles and the School*, Methuen, London & New York.
Delamont, S. (1983), 'The conservative school? Sex roles at home, school and work', in Walker, S. & Barton, L. (eds), *Gender, Class and Education*, Falmer, London.
Ditchburn, G. & Martin, J. (1986), *Education for Girls in the Catholic and Independent Schools in the Western Suburbs of Melbourne and Gippsland*, Victorian Non-government Schools Participation and Equity Program, Victoria.
Dudley, J. & Vidovich, L. (1995), *The Politics of Education: Commonwealth Schools Policy, 1973–1995*, Australian Council for Educational Research, Melbourne.
Dunn, J., Hammonds, B. & Watson, I. (1984), *The All-girls Maths Class at Hawker College*, ACT Schools Authority.
Dusseldorp Skills Forum: *see* Spierings (2003).
Dweck, C. S. (1980), 'Learned helplessness and intellectual achievement' in Garben, J. & Seligman, M. (eds), *Human Helplessness: Theory and Application*, Academic Press, New York.
Elwood, J. & Gipps, C. (1999), *Review of Recent Research on the Achievement of Girls in Single-sex Schools*, Institute of Education, Bedford Way, London.
Encel, S. (1970), *Equality and Authority: A Study of Class, Status and Power in Australia*, Cheshire, Melbourne.
Epstein, D. (eds) (1998), *Failing boys? Issues in Gender and Achievement*, Open University Press, Buckingham (England) & Philadelphia.
Evans, T. (1979), 'Creativity, sex role socialisation and pupil–teacher interactions in early scholing', *Sociological Review*, vol. 27, no. 1, pp. 139–55.
Fairweather, H. (1976), 'Sex differences in cognition', *Cognition*, vol. 4.
Feingold, A. (1988), 'Cognitive gender differences are disappearing', *American Psychologist*, vol. 43, pp. 95–103.
FitzPatrick, J. & Brown, S. (1983), 'Sex-based enrolment patterns in secondary school subjects', *Curriculum Perspectives*, vol. 3, no. 2, pp. 47–52.
Foon, A. (1988), 'The relationship between school type and adolescent self-esteem, attribution styles and affiliation needs: Implications for educational outcomes', *British Journal of Educational Psychology*, vol. 58, pp. 44–54.
Foster, V. (1984), *Changing Choices: Girls, School and Work*, Hale & Iremonger, Sydney.

Friedlander, J. (1985), 'Many girls still feel maths doesn't count', the *Australian*, 17/9/85, p. 10.

Fullarton, S. & Ainley, J. (2000), *Subject Choice by Students in Year 12 in Australian Secondary Schools*, LSAY (Longitudinal Surveys of Australian Youth) Research Report No. 15, Australian Council for Educational Research, Melbourne.

Gilbert, R. & Gilbert, P. (1998), *Masculinity Goes to School*, Allen & Unwin, Sydney.

Gill, J. (1987), 'Self-esteem and girls' schooling' in *Women's Studies Resource Centre Newsletter*, vol. 12, no. 3.

Gill, J. (1992a), Differences in the making: The construction of gender in Australian schooling, Unpublished PhD thesis, University of Adelaide.

Gill, J. (1992b), 'Rephrasing the question: Is single-sex schooling one solution to the equity equation?', *Curriculum Perspectives*, vol. 12, no. 1.

Gill, J. (1995), Commissioned Analysis of Senior Secondary Assessment Board of South Australia (SSABSA).

Gill, J. & Starr, K. (2000), 'Sauce for the goose? Deconstructing the boys-in-education push', *Discourse*, vol. 23, no. 3, pp. 323–33.

Gilligan, C. (1982), *In a Different Voice: Psychological Theory and Women's Development*, Harvard University Press, Cambridge, Massachusetts.

Haag, P. (1998), 'Single-sex education in grades K–12: What does the research tell us?' in *Separated by Sex: A Critical Look at Single-sex Education for Girls*, AAUW Education Foundation/National Education Foundation, Washington DC, p. 18.

Hannan, D., Smyth, E., McCullagh, J., O'Leary, R. & McMahon, D. (1996), *Coeducation and Gender Equity: Exam Performance, Stress and Personal Development*, Oak Tree Press, Dublin.

Hansen, S., Walker, J. & Flom, B. (1995), *Growing Smart: What's Working for Girls*, AAUW Research Report, AAUW Education Foundation, Washington DC, p. 60.

Harding, J. (1981), 'Sex differences in science examinations' in Kelly, A. (ed.), *The Missing Half: Girls and Science Education*, Manchester University Press, Manchester.

Harker, R. & Nash, R. (1997), School type and the education of girls: Coed or girls only?, Paper presented at the annual meeting of the American Educational Research Association, Chicago (ERIC ED410633).

Harris, M. (1986), 'Coeducation and sex roles', *Australian Journal of Education*, vol. 30, no. 2.

Harvey, T. J. (1984), 'Gender differences in subject preference and perception of subject importance among third year secondary pupils in mixed and comprehensive schools', *Educational Studies*, vol. 10, no. 3, pp. 243–53.

Harvey, T. J. (1985), 'Science in single-sex and mixed teaching groups', *Educational Research*, vol. 27, no. 3, pp. 179–82.

Haslem, B. (2002), 'Australia No. 1 for women', the *Australian*, 25/7/02, p. 3.

Hill, M. (2003), Personal communication from the President of the New Zealand Association for Research in Education.

Holz-Ebeling, F., Gratz-Tummers, J. & Schwarz, C. (2000), 'Are boys profiting from coeducation? An empirical study of the significance of coeducation to boys', *Zeitschrift fur Entwicklungpsychologie und Padagogische Psychologie,* vol. 32, no. 2, pp. 94–107.

Horne, R. (2000), The educational performance of males and females in school and tertiary education, Paper presented at the conference titled *Educational Attainment and Labour Market Outcomes,* Department of Education, Training and Youth Affairs, Melbourne.

Howard, S. (1998), 'Candide in the classroom: Self-concept theory and its application', *New Horizons in Education,* no. 98, April, pp. 6–19.

Hubbard, L. & Datnow, A. (2002), 'Are single-sex schools sustainable in the public sector?' in Datnow, A. & Hubbard, L. (eds), *Gender in Policy and Practice: Perspectives on Single-sex and Coeducational Schooling,* RoutledgeFalmer, London.

Hunter, S. (1987), Do schools matter? Gender choice of subjects at single-sex and coeducational schools, Paper presented at an NZARE/AARE conference, Christchurch.

Hutchins School, (1993), *Magenta and Black,* the Newsletter of the Hutchins School, Sandy Bay, Tasmania, p. 4.

Hyde, J., Fennema, E. & Lamon, S. J. (1990), 'Gender differences in mathematics performance: A meta-analysis', *Psychology Bulletin,* vol. 107, pp. 139–55.

IES Conferences (1998), *Improving Outcomes in Boys' Education: Where to Now?,* Proceedings of the 1998 Annual IES Conference, Chatswood, Sydney.

Johnson, L. (1990), *The Modern Girl: Girlhood and Growing Up,* Allen & Unwin, Sydney.

Jones, J. & Young, D. (1995), 'Perceptions of the relevance of mathematics and science: An Australian study', *Research in Science Education,* vol. 25, no. 1, pp. 3–18.

Keeves, J. (1982), *Education and Change in South Australia,* Final Report of the Committee of Enquiry into Education in South Australia, Department of Education, South Australia, Adelaide.

Kelly, A. (1981), *The Missing Half: Girls and Science Education,* Manchester University Press, Manchester.

Kenway, J. (2000), Puzzling about gender, school and post school life: Five paradoxes for policy, Paper presented at the conference titled *Educational Attainment and Labour Market Outcomes,* Department of Education, Training and Youth Affairs, Melbourne.

Kenway, J., Collins, C & McLeod, J. (2000), *Factors Influencing Educational Performance of Males and Females in School and their Initial Destinations after Leaving School,* available at <http://www.dest.gov.au>.

Kenway, J. & Willis, S. (1986), 'Feminist single-sex educational strategies: Some theoretical flaws and practical fallacies', *Discourse,* vol. 7, no. 1, pp. 1–30.

Kessels, U., Hannover, B. & Janetzke, H. (2002), 'High school students' attitudes towards single-sex classes in science', *Psychologie in Erziehung und Unterricht,* vol. 49, no. 1, pp. 17–30.

Kohlberg, L. (1981), *The Philosophy of Moral Development: Moral Stages and the Idea of Justice,* Harper & Row, San Francisco.

Kruse, A. M. (1996), 'Single-sex settings: Pedagogies for girls and boys in

Danish schools' in Murphy, P. & Gipps, G. (eds), *Equity in the Classroom: Towards Effective Pedagogy for Girls and Boys*, Falmer, London, pp. 173–91.

Lamb, S. (1996), *Completing School in the 1990s: Trends in the 1990s*, LSAY (Longitudinal Surveys of Australian Youth) Research Report No. 1, Australian Council for Educational Research, Melbourne.

Lamb, S. (1998), 'Completing school in Australia: Trends in the 1990s.' *Australian Journal of Education*, vol. 42, no. 1, pp. 5–31.

Leder, G. & Forgasz, H. (1997), 'Single-sex classes in a coeducational high school: Highlighting parents' perspectives', *Mathematics Education Research Journal*, vol. 9, no. 3, pp. 274–91.

Lee, V. E. & Marks, H. (1994), 'Sexism in single-sex and coeducational independent secondary school classrooms', *Sociology of Education*, vol. 67, pp. 92–121.

Lee, V. E. & Bryk, A. S. (1986), 'Effects of single-sex secondary schools on student achievement and attitudes', *Journal of Educational Psychology*, vol. 78, pp. 381–95.

Lillico, I. (2002), *Boys and Single-sex Schooling*, available at <http://www.boysforward.com/tips/tip030516.html>.

Lingard, B. & Douglas, P. (1999), *Men Engaging Feminisms: Pro-feminism Backlashes and Schooling*, Open University Press, Buckingham, United Kingdom.

Lorde, A. (1984), *Sister Outsider: Essays and Speeches*, Crossing Press, Freedom, California.

McCalman, J. (1993), *Journeyings: The Biography of a Middle-class Generation 1920–1990*, Melbourne University Press, Carlton, Victoria.

Maccoby, E. (1990), 'Gender and relationships: A developmental account', *American Psychologist*, April, pp. 513–20.

Maccoby, E. & Jacklin, C. (1976), *The Psychology of Sex Differences*, Stanford University Press, Stanford, California.

Mackinnon, A. (1986): *The New Women: Adelaide's Early Women Graduates*, Wakefield Press, Adelaide, South Australia.

McClintock Collective (1988), *Getting into Gear: Gender Inclusive Teaching Strategies in Science*, Curriculum Development Centre, Canberra.

McMillan, J., Hansford, B. & Thurgood, P. (1985), *Single-sex Classes in Coeducational Schools*, Equal Opportunities Unit, Victorian Ministry of Education.

McMillan, J. & Marks, G. (2003), *School Leavers in Australia: Profiles and Pathways*, LSAY (Longitudinal Surveys of Australian Youth) Research Report No. 31, Australian Council for Educational Research, Melbourne.

Mael, F. (1998), Single-sex and coeducational schooling – relationships to socioemotional and academic development', *Review of Educational Research*, vol. 68, no. 2, pp. 101–29.

Marsh, H. W. (1989), 'Effects of attending single-sex and coeducational high schools on achievement, attitudes, behaviours and sex difference', *Journal of Educational Psychology*, vol. 81, pp. 70–85.

Marsh, H. W. & Rowe, K. (1996), 'Effects of single sex and mixed sex mathematics classes within a coeducational school – a reanalysis and comment', *Australian Journal of Education*, vol. 40, no. 2, pp. 147–61.

Marsh, H. W., Smith, I. D., Myers, M. & Owens, L. (1986), The transition from single-sex to coeducation: Effects on academic achievement: A summary report, Paper presented at the conference of the Australian Association for Research in Education, Melbourne.

Marsh, H. W., Smith, I. D., Myers, M. & Owens, L. (1988), 'The transition from single-sex to coeducational high schools: Effects on multiple dimensions of self-concept and on academic achievement', *American Educational Research Journal*, vol. 25, pp. 237–69.

Martin, J. (1972), Sex differences in educational qualifications, in Selleck, R. (ed.), *Melbourne Studies in Education*, Melbourne University Press, Carlton, Victoria.

Martino, W. (1999), ' "Cool boys", "Party animals", "Squids" and "Poofters": Interrogating the dynamics and politics of adolescent masculinities in school', *British Journal of Sociology of Education*, vol. 20, no. 2, pp. 239–63.

Martino, W. & Meyenn, B. (2002), 'War, guns and cool tough things': Interrogating single-sex classes as a strategy for engaging boys in English', *Cambridge Journal of Education*, vol. 32, no. 3, pp. 303–24.

MCEETYA (Ministerial Council on Education, Employment, Training and Youth Affairs) (1993), *National Action Plan for the Education of Girls 1993–97*, Curriculum Corporation, Australian Education Council, Carlton South, Victoria, available at <http://www.curriculum.edu.au/mceetya/public/public.htm#gender>.

MCEETYA (Ministerial Council on Education, Employment, Training and Youth Affairs) (1996), *Gender Equity: A Framework for Australian Schools*, available at <http://www.curriculum.edu.au/mceetya/public/pub336/html>.

MCEETYA (Ministerial Council on Education, Employment, Training and Youth Affairs) (1997), *Gender-Equity Taskforce Gender Equity: A framework for Australian schools*, Canberra: Australian Capital Territory. <http://www.curriculum.edu.au/mceetya/public/public.htm#gender>.

MCEETYA (Ministerial Council for Education, Employment, Training and Youth Affairs) (1999), *The Adelaide Declaration on National Goals for Schooling in the Twenty-First Century*, available at <http://www.curriculum.edu.au/mceetya/nationalgorals/html>.

Miller, P. (1986), *Long Division: State Schooling in South Australian Society*, Wakefield Press, Adelaide, South Australia.

Milligan, S. & Thomson, K. (1992), *Listening to Girls*, A report of the consultancy undertaken for the Review of the National Policy for the Education of Girls in Australian Schools conducted by the Australian Education Council, Curriculum Corporation, Carlton South, Victoria.

Morrow, B. (1991), Effects of gender segregation on female student achievement and attitudes in year eleven mathematics, Unpublished MEd thesis, Latrobe University, Melbourne.

NFER (2002): *see* Spielhofer et al. (2002)

Norton, S. J. & Rennie, L. J. (1997), Is mathematics a male domain? The responses from students in single-sex and coeducational schools, Paper presented at the annual conference of the Australian Association for Research in Education, Brisbane, available at <http://www.aare.edu.au/html>.

Norton, S. J. & Rennie, L. J. (1998), 'Students' attitudes towards mathematics in single-sex and coeducational schools', *Mathematics Education Research Journal*, vol. 10, no. 1, pp. 16–36.

Ormerod, M. (1975), 'Subject preference and choice in single-sex and coeducational secondary schools', *British Journal of Educational Psychology*, vol. 45, pp. 257–67.

Parker, L. H. & Rennie, L. J. (1997), 'Teacher's perceptions of the implementation of single-sex classes in coeducational schools', *Australian Journal of Education*, vol. 41, no. 2, pp. 119–33.

Parker, L. H. & Rennie, L. J. (2002), Teachers' implementation of gender inclusive instructional strategies in single-sex and mixed sex science classrooms. *International Journal of Science Education*, vol. 24, no. 9, pp. 881–97.

Peck, B. & Trimmer, K. (1994), Gender differences in tertiary entrance scores, Paper presented at the annual conference of the Australian Association for Research in Education, Newcastle, available at <http://www.aare.edu.au/html>.

Phillips, M. (2002), 'The lie that betrays boys', the *Sunday Mail*, 25/08/02, p. 90.

Phillips, S. (1980), *Young Australians: The Attitudes of Our Children*, Harper & Row, Sydney.

Praetz, H. (1983), *Education and Employment: Patterns of Participation of Victorian 15–19 Year Olds*, VISE Report, Victorian Institute of Secondary Education, Melbourne.

Ramsay, E., Tranter, D., Charlton, S. & Sumner, R. (1998), *Higher Education Access and Equity*, EIP Report, Department of Education, Training and Youth Affairs.

Rennie, L. J. & Parker, L. H. (1997), 'Students' and teachers' perceptions of single-sex and mixed-sex mathematics classes', *Mathematics Education Research Journal*, vol. 9, no. 3, pp. 257–73.

Riordan, C. (1998), 'The future of single-sex schools' in *Separated by Sex: A Critical Look at Single-sex Education for Girls*, AAUW Education Foundation/National Education Foundation, Washington DC, p. 53.

Riordan, C. (2002), 'What do we know about the effects of single-sex schools in the private sector? Implications for public schools' in Datnow, A. & Hubbard, L. (eds) (2002), *Gender in Policy and Practice: Perspectives on Single-sex and Coeducational Schooling*, RoutledgeFalmer, London.

Rogers, L. (1999), *Sexing the Brain*, Weidenfeld & Nicolson, London.

Roper, T. (1971), *The Myth of Equality*, Heineman Educational, Melbourne.

Rost, D. H. & Pruisken, C. (2000), 'Together weak? Separated strong? Girls and coeducation', *Zeitschrift fur Padagogische Psychologie*. vol. 14, no. 4, pp. 177–93.

Rowe, K. (1988), 'Single-sex and mixed classes: The effects of class type on student achievement, confidence and participation in mathematics', *Australian Journal of Education*, vol. 32, no. 2, pp. 180–202.

Rowe, K., Nix, P. & Tepper, G. (1986), Single-sex versus mixed-sex classes: The joint effects of gender and class type on student performance in and attitudes towards mathematics, Paper presented at the conference of the Australian Association for Research in Education, Melbourne.

Sadker, M. & Sadker, D. (1994), *Failing at Fairness: How America's Schools Cheat Girls*, Macmillan, New York.

Shaw, J. (1981), 'Education and the individual: Schooling for girls or mixed schooling – a mixed blessing?' in Deem, R. (ed.), *Schooling for Women's Work*, Routledge & Kegan Paul, London.

Smith, A. (1985), Sex differences in student perceptions of people in charge, Presentation to the Delissa Research Institute, University of South Australia.

Smith, I. (1975), 'Sex differences in the self-concept of primary school children', *Australian Psychologist*, vol. 10, no. 1.

Smith, I. (1996), *Gender differentiation: Gender Differences in Academic Achievement and Self-concept in Coeducational and Single-sex Schools*, Final report of the Australian Research Council project, available at <http://alex.edfac.usyd.edu.au/LocalResource/Study1/coed.html>.

Spender, D. (1982), *Invisible Women: The Schooling Scandal*, Writers and Readers, London.

Spender, D. (1980), 'Disappearing tricks' in Spender, D. & Sarah, E. (eds), *Learning to Lose: Sexism and Education*, The Women's Press, London.

Spender, D. & Sarah, E. (eds), *Learning to Lose: Sexism and Education*, The Women's Press, London.

Spielhofer, T., O'Donnell, L., Benton, T., Schagen, S. & Schagen, I. (2002), *The Impact of School Size and Single-sex Education on Performance*, LSAY (Longitudinal Surveys of Australian Youth) Research Report No. 33, NFER, Slough, United Kingdom.

Spierings, J. (2003), *How Young People are Faring 2003*, an update about the learning and work situation of young Australians, Dusseldorp Skills Forum, Sydney, available at <http://www.dsf.org.au/papers/html>.

Stanworth, M. (1982), *Gender and Schooling: A Study of Sexual Division in the Classroom*, Hutchinson, London.

Starr, K. (1999), That roar which lies on the other side of silence: An analysis of women principals' responses to structural reform in South Australian education, Unpublished PhD thesis, University of South Australia.

Steedman, J. (1983), *Examination Results in Mixed and Single-sex Schools: Findings from the National Child Development Study*, Equal Opportunities Commission, Manchester, United Kingdom.

Stent, P. & Gillies, R. M. (2000), 'Occupational attitudes and expectations of year 12 students in single-sex and coeducational schools: A focus on female youth', *Australian Journal of Career Development*, vol. 9, no. 3, pp.13–19.

Stewart, G. (1998), *Improving Outcomes in Boys' Education: Where to Now?*, Proceedings of the 1998 Annual IES Conference, Chatswood, Sydney.

Strober, M. & Tyack, D. (1980), 'Why do women teach and men manage? A report on research in schools', *Signs*, vol. 5, no. 3, pp. 494–503.

Teese, R. & Polesel, J. (2003), *Undemocratic Schooling: Equity and Quality in Mass Secondary Education in Australia*, Melbourne University Publishing, Carlton, Victoria.

Teese, R., Davies, M., Charlton, M. & Polesel, J. (1995), *Who Wins at School? Boys and Girls in Australian Secondary Education*, Department of Education Policy and Management, University of Melbourne, Melbourne.

Towns, D. (1985), *The Responsibility to Educate Girls for a Technologically Oriented Society*, Deakin University Press, Geelong, Victoria.

Townsend, G. (2002), quoted by Ebru Yaman in 'Gender trials put boys in a class by themselves', the *Australian*, 02/09/02, p. 13.

US Department of Education, Office of Educational Research and Improvement (1992), Single-sex schooling: Perspectives from practices and research, Unpublished paper cited in Haag, P. (2002), 'Single sex education in grades K–12' in *The Jossey Bass Reader on Gender and Education*, John Wiley & Sons, New York.

Victorian Commission into Equal Opportunity in Schools (1977), *Report*, Premier's Department, Government of Victoria.

West, P. (2000), *Submission to the Inquiry into the Education of Boys*, available at <http://www.menshealth.uws.edu.au/Documents/InquiryBoysEd.html>.

West, P. (1988), Boys, sport and schooling: The popular debate and some recent research, Paper delivered at *Improving Outcomes in Boys' Education: Where to Now?*, the 1998 Annual IES Conference, Chatswood, Sydney.

Willingham, W. W., Cole, N. S., Lewis, C. & Leung, S. W. (1997), 'Test performance' in Willingham, W. W. & Cole, N. S., *Gender and Fair Assessment*, Lawrence Erlbaum Associates, Mahwah, New Jersey.

Willis, S. (1989), *'Real Girls Don't Do Maths': Gender and the Construction of Privilege*, Deakin University Press, Geelong, Victoria.

Woodward, L .J., Fergusson, D. M. & Horwood, L. J. (1999), 'Effects of single-sex and coeducational schooling on children's academic achievement', *Australian Journal of Education*, vol. 43, no. 2, pp. 142–56.

Woolf, Virginia (1977, originally published in 1929), *A Room of One's Own*, Grafton Books, London.

Yates, J. & Firkin, J. (1986), *Student Participation in Mathematics: Gender Differences in the Last Decade*, Victorian Curriculum and Assessment Board, Melbourne.

Yates, L. (1996), Who are girls and what are we doing to them in schools? Keynote address to the *Schooldays Conference*, Magill Campus, University of South Australia.

Yates, L. (1993), *The Education of Girls: Policy, Research and the Question of Gender*, Australian Council for Educational Research, Melbourne.

Yates, S. M. (2001), 'Students' achievements and perceptions of school climate during the transition from single-sex to coeducation', *International Education Journal*, vol. 2, no.4, pp. 317–28.

Yates, S. M. (2002), 'Stepping from single to mixed sex education: Boys' progress and perceptions during the restructuring', *International Education Journal*, vol. 3, no. 4, pp. 23–33.

Young, D. (1994), 'Single-sex schools and science achievement: Are girls really advantaged?', *International Journal of Science Education*, vol. 16, no. 3, pp. 315–25

INDEX